SKINNY GRILLING

by BARBARA GRUNES

Surrey Books
CHICAGO

SKINNY GRILLING is published by Surrey Books, Inc.,
230 E. Ohio St., Suite 120, Chicago, IL 60611.

First edition: 1 2 3 4 5

This book is manufactured in the United States of America.

Library of Congress Cataloging-in-Publication data:

Grunes, Barbara.
   Skinny grilling / by Barbara Grunes. — 1st ed.
   200 p.   cm.
   Includes index.
   ISBN 0-940625-67-9 (pbk.) : $12.95
   1. Barbecue cookery. 2. Low-fat diet—Recipes.   I. Title.
TX840.B3G793 1995
641.5'784—dc20

94-39293
CIP

Editorial and production: *Bookcrafters, Inc., Chicago*
Art director: *Hughes & Co., Chicago*
Cover and interior illustrations by *Laurel DiGangi*
Back cover photos courtesy *National Live Stock and Meat Board*

For free catalog and prices on quantity purchases, contact Surrey Books at the
address above.

This title is distributed to the trade by Publishers Group West.

Other Titles in the "Skinny" Cookbooks Series:

Skinny Beef
Skinny Chicken
Skinny Chocolate
Skinny Cookies, Cakes & Sweets
Skinny One-Pot Meals
Skinny Pasta

Skinny Pizzas
Skinny Potatoes
Skinny Sauces & Marinades
Skinny Seafood
Skinny Soups
Skinny Spices

This book is dedicated to my son, Louis Kraus, M.D.,
and to Joanna Gutman, Michele and Dick Chroman,
David Marion, and Patty Kolasinski for all of their
good advice, tastings, testing, and caring.

CONTENTS

WHY "SKINNY" GRILLING?

L et's face it: Americans are absolutely crazy about grilling. As a matter of fact, as I write these very words, the charwood briquettes on my own grill are well on their way to becoming a glowing body of cooking coals. Nearly nine out of ten American households own and use grills, and every day, on an average, over six million American grills are fired up on patios, in backyards, on fire escapes and balconies, on decks and porches—wherever there's space in yards, trailer parks, public parks, beaches, even inside kitchens on stove-top grills.

Grilling is by far the most popular cooking method in America because it is such a social activity. Grilling embodies a quality of both fun and participation; it is communal, informal, and combines a sense of picnic and party. Grilling is an open, exhibitive form of cooking, where all can share in and enjoy the flashes, sizzles, aromas, and great expectation of a feast. Typically, grilling takes cooking out of the kitchen and into the open spaces, into the spring, summer, or fall air, and all aspects of the meal take on more of the flavor of a celebration than of routine daily life.

Another phenomenon in American life is that, by the thousands, we have become more concerned about what we eat, about how our food is prepared and cooked, about the effect of what we consume in our bodies and lives. Americans no longer have their eyes focused solely on alluring foods and recipes but increasingly upon *healthy* foods and recipes. Widespread awareness of the risks of high-fat and high-sodium diets, about the nutritive value of various foods, about the body's ability to process and use fats, carbohydrates, and fiber has drastically changed and reshaped American eating habits.

This combination, the love of grilling and the desire for healthy eating, has motivated the creation of this book. It has been my consistent commitment during the development and testing of these recipes to provide the reader with the finest and healthiest ingredients that garden or grocer can provide, that cook can prepare, and that grill can produce—without sacrificing the slightest degree of texture, taste, or enjoyment.

Today, more than ever before, Americans desire and seek simplicity and quickness in grilling recipes, not so much in the amount of time that food is on the grill, for that is generally a pleasurable and relaxing time, but in the amount of time and effort involved in preparing food for the grill. In a society where time is increasingly precious, home cooks have little inclination to spend hours on food preparation. Yet we increasingly desire new and unique recipes and food combinations. To meet this interesting blend of desires, I have striven to develop simple, easy to prepare recipes for the grill—yet recipes that are unique, inspiring, and fun.

Traditionally, American grilling has mainly consisted of throwing fatty chunks of meat on the grill, maybe ladling on some high-sodium barbecue sauce, and serving the result with a baked potato smothered in butter and sour cream. Without disparaging our tastes, this book stands as a refutation to that high-fat, high-calorie, high-sodium tradition. Very simply, "Skinny Grilling" means *healthy* grilling. It is the constant focus of this book to present recipes that are not only "good from the grill" but recipes that are "good for you from the grill."

The Nutritional Data

Specific nutritional information is provided for each recipe in this book, but please remember that nutritional data are rarely—if ever—infallible. The recipe analyses were derived using software highly regarded by nutritionists and dietitians. Figures are based on actual lab values of ingredients rather than general rules of thumb, such as each fat gram contains 9 calories, so our results might vary from the results of traditional formulas.

Other factors affecting the nutritional data include: the variable sizes of meat cuts, vegetables, and fruits; a plus or minus 20 percent error factor on the nutritional labels of packaged foods; and cooking techniques and appliances. Thus, if you have any health problems that mandate strict dietary requirements, it is important to consult a physician, clinical dietitian, or nutritionist before proceeding with any recipe in this book. Also, if you are a diabetic or require a diet that restricts calories, fat, or sodium remember that the nutritional analysis figures may be accurate for the recipe we tested but not for the food you cooked due to the variables.

Please also note that ingredients listed as "optional" are not included in the nutritional data, and if seasonings are used "to taste," the data may become skewed. When alternate choices of ingredients are given, as "vegetable stock, *or* chicken stock," the first-listed item is the one used to develop the nutritional data.

In summary, use the nutritional data as a starting point for planning healthier meals, but regard the figures more as guidelines than as components of an immutable formula.

Flavor and Health

Skinny Grilling recipes constantly, yet subtly, focus on reduced fat, sodium, and fewer calories while retaining all the taste and fulfilling the fun expectations of grilled food. While the recipes consistently call for the leanest cuts of meat, poultry, and seafood, tenderness, juiciness, and taste are preserved and enhanced by preparing and grilling meats using a variety of low-fat rubs, marinades, brushing sauces, mops, and some terrific fruit- and vegetable-based sauces. The book emphasizes the use of fresh herb and wood aromatics to create flavorful, succulent, and complementary tastes.

These recipes also supplement traditional grilled foods with grilled fresh fruits and vegetables. Where possible, I have recommended low-fat cheeses and call for margarine in lieu of butter. The book also includes several new and entertaining grilling methods, including the use of herb stems as skewers, and grilling thin slices of fish directly on top of fresh fruits and vegetables.

So, here it is, *Skinny Grilling,* the key to looking and feeling good in your own backyard while you savor the enticing aromas of the grill and await the repast.

1.
THE ART OF GRILLING

Grilling meat must certainly have been the earliest of all cooking
methods, and its discovery probably was an accident. On the
periphery of a smoldering prairie fire, a lightning fire, primitive man
found the remains of animals that had not been able to escape the blaze.
The delicious aroma of cooked meat, the increased flavor and juiciness of
the feast, and the heightened tenderness must have lit the bulb of
inspiration, as the consumption of grilled food began its irreversible
progress from a survival skill to a culinary art.

Direct and Indirect Grilling

While myriad designs, shapes, and styles of grills are available on the
market today, there are actually only two ways to grill: direct (or open)

grilling, which is done directly above the bed of coals or heat source; and indirect (or closed) grilling, which is not done directly above the coals, and a cover or hood is used to shield the food from the open air.

Direct Grilling is the most common way to grill, and it is recommended for most foods. It uses radiation to cook, the heat rising from the glowing coals to be absorbed by the food. It can be done using either open or closed grills. Direct grilling takes place at higher temperatures and more quickly than indirect grilling. Flare-ups are common if the grill is uncovered, so watch food carefully and douse flare-ups immediately.

If you are grilling foods that require different cooking temperatures, you can create two grilling areas on opposite sides of the grill by piling more coals in one area of the fire pan than in the other. Cook foods that require lower temperatures on one side and higher-temperature foods on the other. Also, you can move foods that are cooking too quickly to the lower-temperature side of the grill at any time.

The main advantage of direct grilling is that foods can be cooked very quickly, and moisture and flavor can be retained in the leanest cuts of meat. The outer surfaces of foods will sear, sealing in the natural juices.

Indirect Grilling should be done only on grills that are covered. It employs convection as its heating method. Heated air and smoke circulate constantly about the food, transferring heat and cooking the food evenly. At the lower temperatures of indirect grilling, both meats and vegetables absorb the flavors of marinades and sauces, and the taste of grilled foods is further enhanced by the smoky flavor that permeates them, particularly when cooked with hardwood charcoal or wood chips and aromatics (see "Fuels," below).

Indirect grilling is an ideal cooking method for larger pieces of meat, roasts, whole birds, and foods requiring longer cooking times and less intense heat than afforded by direct grilling. Arrange the coals on opposite sides of the fire pan, leaving the center area open. A drip pan may be placed between the hot-coal mounds to collect drippings from the grilling food. The drip pan may be filled with water, diluted wine, broth, or fruit juices to create moist heat and to add subtle flavors to the food. Aromatic herbs may be added periodically to the liquid in the drip pan for additional flavoring. You may have to add additional coals during an extended cooking process. Remember to keep the grill covered during indirect grilling.

Types of Grills

Today, there are almost as many types of grills on the market as there are venues for grilling. Your choices range from stripped-down tabletop models to permanently installed behemoths that cost hundreds of dollars. Here, we've broken grills down into seven generic categories, which hopefully will give you some basis for comparison.

Kettle Grills have covers that fit over large, rounded cooking chambers. Most kettle grills have one or several sets of dampers, or vents, that control the heat. Heat is reflected off the round chamber and cover of the kettle, creating a natural convection oven effect. The cover of a kettle grill can be left off for open grilling.

Hooded Grills are similar to kettle grills in that a hinged cover traps heat for convection grilling and intensifies the smoky flavor imparted to foods. Hooded grills are square or rectangular in shape, and, unlike most kettle grills, they often offer adjustable cooking grids and fuel grates, which enable the cook to control grilling temperature. Like the kettle grill, the hooded grill may be left open for open grilling.

Braziers, or open grills, do not have hoods. They are generally the least expensive and simplest form of grill. Braziers can be either round or rectangular. Some braziers are more elaborate, having a half-hood or hinged hood and a windscreen. Braziers are light, mobile, and easy to use and can be great for casual backyard get-togethers, block parties, or picnics where grill mobility is an advantage. If you are purchasing a brazier, be careful that the unit you buy is sturdy and is supported by solid legs.

Water Smoker Grills have a cylindrical shape that encourages smoke to rise toward the food. A water pan is used to keep the food moist through the evaporation process. Aromatics can be added to the water or sprinkled atop the charcoal or hardwood fuel. Water smokers are designed to cook large items, such as a turkey or a roast, over many hours, so it is important to replenish charcoal and water as necessary. For a makeshift smoker, you can convert a kettle grill by piling coals along one side only and placing a pan of water on the opposite side. This should work for smaller food items that do not require lengthy smoking. (See recipes for smoked foods in Chapter 7.)

Portable, or Tabletop, Grills are small, highly mobile, and very popular for family outings, picnics, days at the beach, and camping. Portable grills are very convenient for grilling for one or two persons. They are available in small kettle or brazier styles and can be used for either open or closed grilling.

Indoor Stove-Top Grills are a relatively new and convenient idea. They sit directly on the range burners and do an admirable job. They are especially appreciated in winter or on rainy days. Be sure to use them according to individual manufacturer's directions, as they can be hazardous inside the home.

Gas and Electric Grills are increasingly popular because of the convenience of having a fire at the push of a button. Gas grills are fueled by either liquid propane (LP) gas or natural gas. The burning gas heats artificial briquettes. Electric grills employ a heating element located beneath a grate of artificial briquettes. Both gas and electric grills are convenient and efficient although they provide less natural flavor and less ambiance than charcoal grills.

Fuels

The term "charcoal" has become embroiled in a controversy of definition in recent years. The item that is most common and most widely sold bearing the label "Charcoal Briquettes" may in reality consist of low-grade coal, wood ash, and petroleum products bound together by chemical additives. Such briquettes may be very expensive, but it is my strong recommendation to steer clear; they can give food a distinctly unpleasant taste and coat foods with a greasy residue. These popular briquettes burn considerably faster than wood-based briquettes and may not be nearly as economical as they seem.

Hardwood Charcoal, or Charwood, is made by slowly smoldering whole pieces of wood, often cherry, maple, oak, hickory, or mesquite, in a low-oxygen fire. The wood is reduced to a carbon product without fillers or additives. Hardwood charcoal burns hot and cleanly, and rather than leaving an unpleasant taste in foods, it imparts a very pleasant flavor. It also is slow burning. I highly recommend seeking out hardwood charcoal for your grilling purposes.

Hardwood Chunks can be used very effectively for grilling. Most fruit woods and hickory, ash, oak, alder, and mesquite make excellent grilling fuel. Be sure that the wood you use is dry. Wood chunks won't burn nearly as hot as charcoal yet will burn more quickly than charcoal, so you must time your cooking accordingly. However, each type of wood will provide its own delightful flavor to the grilled food. Avoid using resinous woods, such as fir or pine, which give food a very unpleasant taste.

Aromatics are not actually a grilling fuel in themselves, but they make absolutely outstanding flavor additives. Sometimes referred to as flavor, or smoking, chips, wood aromatics such as cherry, apple, maple, grapevine, olive, and mesquite can be gently tossed—in the form of twigs or chips—onto the coals in a closed grill to add distinctive tastes and flavors to grilling food. Aromatics should be soaked in water before being distributed evenly and periodically during the cooking process over the hot coals. Aromatics are of little use with open grills as the smoke disperses too quickly to flavor the food.

Fresh or dried herbs also make excellent aromatic additives and can be tossed on coals to lightly flavor food. Bay leaves, fennel, savory, rosemary, sage, thyme, and tarragon are especially effective for delicately flavoring poultry and fish.

Cooking Temperatures

Be sure to allow plenty of time for your coals to reach the right stage for grilling. I suggest that you allot 30 to 45 minutes to ensure that you do not become hurried and attempt to grill on coals that are not thoroughly lit or coals that are too hot. When your coals are red hot and glowing, you will not be able to hold your palm 6 inches above them for more than 3 seconds. That is still too hot for most grilling.

When the coals have become covered by a layer of gray ash and you can hold your palm about 6 inches above them for around 5 seconds, the fire is medium hot. Most grilling is done over medium-hot coals. If you are cooking a roast or a whole bird or large fish, you may want to use low heat, when all of the red glow is gone and you can hold your hand comfortably over the coals. However, be certain that your fire has not gone out entirely and that you have not lost most of your grilling heat. If the heat seems too low, try opening the vents to supply oxygen and reinvigorate the coals.

Remember that heat and grilling time will vary considerably, depending on a number of factors, particularly the condition of your coals. Be careful to monitor the grilling process frequently, both at high and at lower temperatures.

Grilling Accessories

An Electric Starter may seem like a rather expensive luxury, but it is a safe and very effective way to start fuel. Its long life makes it more economical than starter fluid in the long run. The main disadvantage is that the electric starter requires a nearby electric outlet. Nestle the starter among the coals and plug it in. The starter heats to red hot and ignites the coals around it, which spread the fire to other coals.

A Grill Chimney is a metal cylindrical with two separated chambers inside and vents on the sides or bottom. Fill the top section of the chimney with briquettes, and stuff a crumpled piece of newspaper in the bottom section. Place the chimney on the grate of your grill and light the newspaper. When ignited, empty the coals into the firepan.

Liquid Starters are the most commonly used charcoal starters, but they are also the most expensive, the most dangerous, the least environmentally friendly, and they often impart an unpleasant flavor to grilled food. Liquid starters seem convenient, but they have virtually no other redeeming factor.

Insulated Pot Holders and a good quality, extended-sleeve, fireproof mitt are an obvious must for grilling. Be sure that your mitt and pot holders are available near the grill at all times and that you have not inadvertently carried them away from the grill area.

Long-Handled Tongs serve as an all-purpose tool at the grill and will handle a multitude of duties. Use them to move coals when necessary or to turn food on the grill. Other long-handled cooking tools, such as a spatula, a fork, and a spoon, are also handy, but a good pair of tongs can effectively perform most jobs. If you use a grill fork, be careful not to pierce meat and poultry as it grills or it will release precious juices.

Basting Brushes come in many shapes, sizes, and bristle widths, but at least one good long-handled basting brush, preferably with a 45-degree bend near the bristles, is necessary for brushing on marinades and sauces. I suggest having several brushes available in the event you are using a variety of coatings.

Skewers. Sooner or later you will certainly make kabobs. At least one set of skewers will be necessary for successful kabobs, whether meat, vegetables, poultry, fish, fruit, or any combination of the above. Wooden or bamboo skewers are excellent and attractive for light, short, or mid-sized kabob combinations and quick-cooking foods. Soak wooden or bamboo skewers in water before use so that they will not burn while grilling.

Double-pronged and single metal skewers also work admirably with most foods, and they are particularly effective for grilling heavy chunks of meat or for long-skewered dishes. Be absolutely certain to use a mitt or pot holder when turning hot metal skewers or when removing them from the grill. Double-pronged skewers are available at some cooking stores, and they are great for preventing food from shifting while turning. You can also thread kabobs onto two single skewers to create the same handy effect.

A Spray Bottle of water is very useful for dousing flare-ups when you are open grilling.

A Meat Thermometer of good quality will pay for itself, and it will take the guess work, and potential disappointment, out of grilling roasts, whole birds, and other meats and poultry. Meat thermometers do not work with thinner cuts of meat.

A Grill-Side Carving Board or wooden platter, preferably with a juice canal, will be a constant asset.

A Wire Brush is an essential clean-up tool. The cooking grid or rack should be scraped clean before each grill use. Treat your grill grid as you would a frying pan or your oven shelves. Do not attempt to grill on a grease- and food-coated grid or your food may pick up unpleasant tastes and stick to the grid or rack. Clean your grill brush by washing it out with hot water to remove grease and food particles.

A Grill Basket with a hinged lid is very valuable for grilling and turning small pieces of meat, light vegetables, shellfish, and fish fillets. The food can be cooked in the grill basket, which serves to prevent pieces from falling through the grid onto the coals.

It is both wise and convenient to keep a flashlight and a fire extinguisher close by your grill. If you need either, you will be extremely thankful to have it available.

Tips for Happy and Successful Grilling

Remember that when using any grilling recipe, including those in this book, many variables make grilling an inexact culinary art. Grilling times vary greatly depending on type of food, combinations of foods, thickness of food, temperature, quantity, distribution of coals, distance between cooking surface and coals, and other factors such as wind velocity and type of grill. The best advice is to be attentive while grilling: watch the food as it cooks. Make adjustments as necessary, such as adding charcoal, spreading hot coals, adjusting vents, moving foods to cooler areas of the grill—whatever is necessary to ensure successful cooking.

Always begin grilling on a clean grill. Clean both the grill grid or rack and the ash-catcher. A full ash-catcher will inhibit the flow of oxygen around the coals.

Be sure to allow coals to reach the proper condition and temperature before you begin grilling. Do not attempt to grill over coals that are too hot or too cool. Thoroughly preheat the cooking surface. Food will stick to a grid that is merely warm.

To prevent food from sticking, you may lightly oil or spray the grilling surface before you begin to cook. If you brush or rub oil onto the grill grid, be careful not to burn yourself or to drop oil onto hot coals.

Before you begin to grill, be sure that you have all the necessary tools—your mitt, platters, and other accessories—at hand.

Position your grill in a safe area, away from your house or garage and away from overhanging tree limbs. If necessary, rake the area around the grill to prevent a spark from causing a fire. Keep the grill away from your car or any flammables.

Never use a grill indoors unless it is specifically designed and intended for indoor grilling. Keep children and pets well away from a hot grill. Always use a mitt or pot holders when operating a grill.

Allow the grill to cool down thoroughly after cooking. To extinguish the fire, cover the grill and close the vents; douse the coals of an open grill. Never leave a hot grill unattended.

Feel free to experiment and adapt grilling recipes for your own purposes and enjoyment. Use your imagination and enjoy fully the manifold capabilities of your grill. Have fun and enjoy.

2.
APPETIZERS

Bruschetta

Salmon Fingers with Basil Aroma

Wood-Smoked Pizza

Grilled Quesadillas with Papaya Salsa

Chicken Satay with Peanut Sauce

Turkey Sausage with Sweet Peppers

Soft-Shell Crabs with Yogurt Chili Sauce

Turkey Mini-Burgers

Grilled Portobello Mushrooms

BRUSCHETTA

*From the hills above Florence, Italy, comes this easy
and delicious appetizer.*

Makes 8 servings

Onion Topping

Olive-oil-flavored non-stick cooking spray
2 cups thin-sliced onion
¾ cup chopped celery
1 cup chopped yellow or red tomatoes
3 tablespoons capers, including 1 tablespoon
liquid
½ teaspoon salt
¼ teaspoon pepper

Brushing Mixture

4 cloves garlic, mashed
2 tablespoons olive oil
8 slices Italian or French bread

First prepare the onion topping. Heat a sprayed non-stick frying pan. Sauté onions and celery, covered, over medium heat for 5 minutes or until tender; stir occasionally. Add tomatoes, capers, salt, and pepper. Reheat to serve.

Brushing Mixture: Mix together garlic and olive oil. Brush bread lightly on both sides with oil mixture.

Spray grill rack and place on grid over ashen-hot coals. Toast bread on both sides. Remove from heat and top with onion mixture. Serve hot.

Nutritional Data

PER SERVING		EXCHANGES	
Calories	143	Milk	0.0
% Calories from fat	29	Veg.	1.0
Fat (gm)	4.7	Fruit	0.0
Sat. Fat (gm)	0.7	Bread	1.0
Cholesterol (mg)	0	Meat	0.0
Sodium (mg)	384	Fat	1.0
Protein (gm)	3.5		
Carbohydrate (gm)	22.6		

SALMON FINGERS WITH BASIL AROMA

For aroma, scatter ½ cup rinsed and drained dried basil over the hot coals just as you are about to grill.

Makes 6 servings

1 lb. center-cut salmon fillet, boned, skinned
½ cup dry white wine
¼ cup fine whole-wheat breadcrumbs
  Non-stick cooking spray
½ cup dried basil for aromatic
4 lettuce leaves, wash and pat dry
1 cup chopped tomatoes

Cut salmon into 1-inch strips. Soak salmon strips in a shallow dish with wine for 1 hour, turning once. Drain.

Roll salmon fingers in breadcrumbs.

Spray a grill rack and place it on grid over ashen-hot coals. Scatter rinsed and drained basil over coals.

Grill salmon, turning once with a long-handled spatula. Grill fish about 4 minutes on each side or until it is done to taste. Salmon will flake easily when tested with a fork.

To serve, place salmon fingers on a salad plate over lettuce leaves. Spoon on chopped tomatoes next to the salmon. Serve hot or cold.

Nutritional Data

PER SERVING		EXCHANGES	
Calories	108	Milk	0.0
% Calories from fat	24	Veg.	1.0
Fat (gm)	2.9	Fruit	0.0
Sat. Fat (gm)	0.6	Bread	0.0
Cholesterol (mg)	13.6	Meat	1.5
Sodium (mg)	82	Fat	0.0
Protein (gm)	11.8		
Carbohydrate (gm)	5.2		

WOOD-SMOKED PIZZA

Chicago is famous for its deep-dish pizza made with a cornmeal crust. This pizza is also made with a cornmeal crust, which yields a denser, richer crust. You can substitute white cornmeal if you wish.

Makes 8 servings

Crust

    1 cup, scant, warm water
    ½ teaspoon honey
    1 pkg. (2½ teaspoons) active dry yeast
    2 cups bread flour
    ¾ cups yellow cornmeal
    ½ teaspoon salt
    2 tablespoons olive oil

Topping

    4 teaspoons olive oil
    4 large, ripe garden tomatoes, sliced thin
    4 cloves garlic, minced
    ½ teaspoon salt
    2 tablespoons each: fresh basil, oregano, chives,
       and parsley
    4 tablespoons crumbled, skim mozzarella cheese

Crust: In a glass or small bowl mix water with honey. Sprinkle yeast over water and stir until yeast dissolves. Yeast will begin to bubble in about 5 minutes.

While yeast is "proofing," mix flour, cornmeal, salt, and oil. Use either an electric mixer, food processor, or a bowl and wooden spoon. Stir in yeast and process only a few seconds if using a processor, and 3 to 5 minutes if using an electric mixer. Dough may be sticky.

Place dough in a bowl, and cover lightly with plastic wrap or a damp towel. Let dough rise about 1 hour or until double in size. Punch dough down, and let it stand for 5 minutes.

Knead dough on a lightly floured board or on a pastry cloth for a few minutes until smooth and shiny.

Let dough rise again for about 40 minutes, and again punch it down.

Stretch and shape dough by hand, or use a rolling pin on a lightly floured board. Shape dough into four 7-inch circles or free-form shapes.

Topping: Brush dough with oil. Arrange tomato slices on top and sprinkle with spices, herbs, and cheese.

Using a spatula or pizza paddle sprinkled with cornmeal, put pizzas onto preheated tiles placed on a baking sheet. Place over ashen-hot coals. Cover grill, and cook pizzas until done to taste, about 5 to 6 minutes. Turn pizzas around once during grilling. Crusts will color slightly.

Remove pizzas with long-handled spatula or paddle. Cut each into serving pieces and serve hot. Sprinkle pizzas with red pepper flakes if desired.

Nutritional Data

PER SERVING		EXCHANGES	
Calories	245	Milk	0.0
% Calories from fat	27	Veg.	1.0
Fat (gm)	7.4	Fruit	0.0
Sat. Fat (gm)	1.3	Bread	2.0
Cholesterol (mg)	2	Meat	0.0
Sodium (mg)	294	Fat	1.5
Protein (gm)	7		
Carbohydrate (gm)	38.2		

GRILLED QUESADILLAS WITH PAPAYA SALSA

Quesadillas are a Mexican dish you can serve as a sandwich or as an appetizer.

Makes 6 servings

Salsa

  1 cup chopped tomatoes
  1 cup chopped, peeled papaya
  ½ cup chopped onion
  1 jalapeño pepper, carefully seeded and chopped
  2 tablespoons fresh lime juice
  ¼ cup chopped cilantro

Quesadillas

  3 small (6–7 in.) flour tortillas
  2¼ cups fat-free ricotta cheese
  3 tablespoons grated skim mozzarella cheese
  ¾ cup cooked, mashed, and cooled pinto beans
  1 teaspoon ground cumin

First prepare the salsa. Combine all salsa ingredients in a small bowl. Cover and refrigerate until ready to serve. Toss ingredients before serving.

Quesadillas: To make each quesadilla, spread ¾ cup of ricotta cheese over one-half of each tortilla. Sprinkle with 1 tablespoon of mozzarella cheese. Mix mashed beans with cumin, and sprinkle ¼ cup of it over the cheese. Fold each tortilla in half, pressing halves together lightly with your finger tips.

Spray a grill rack and adjust it on the grid over ashen-hot coals. Place quesadillas on rack, and grill until each side begins to brown, turning once. Using a pair of kitchen scissors, cut each quesadilla in half to serve.

Nutritional Data

PER SERVING		EXCHANGES	
Calories	184	Milk	0.0
% Calories from fat	8	Veg.	1.0
Fat (gm)	1.7	Fruit	0.0
Sat. Fat (gm)	0.6	Bread	1.5
Cholesterol (mg)	12.1	Meat	1.5
Sodium (mg)	75	Fat	0.0
Protein (gm)	18.5		
Carbohydrate (gm)	27.9		

CHICKEN SATAY WITH PEANUT SAUCE

Chicken satay is a popular Indonesian delicacy that is grilled on skewers.

Makes 8 servings

Peanut Sauce (about 1 cup)

    Non-stick cooking spray
- ¼ cup chopped green onion
- 3 cloves garlic, minced
- 1 teaspoon grated fresh ginger, *or* ½ teaspoon ginger powder
- ½ teaspoon ground cumin
- ½ teaspoon cayenne pepper
- ¼ teaspoon salt
- 2 tablespoons light soy sauce
- 2 tablespoons dark corn syrup
- 2 tablespoons fresh lemon juice
- 3 tablespoons light, low sodium peanut butter
- 2 tablespoons coconut milk

Chicken
- 2 chicken breasts, about 32 ozs., bones and skin discarded
- 8 short bambo skewers, soaked in water 2 minutes, drained

Peanut Sauce: Spray a small non-stick saucepan. Sauté onions, garlic, and ginger, covered, about 3 minutes over medium heat. Stir as needed. Add cumin, pepper, and salt.

Put mixture into a food processor or blender, add remaining ingredients, and puree. Spoon sauce into bowl. Cover and refrigerate until needed. You can make sauce the day before it's served.

Chicken: Cut in thin lengthwise strips and pound chicken. Thread strips onto drained skewers.

Spray a grill rack and adjust it on grid over ashen-hot coals. Grill chicken about 2 minutes on each side, turning as necessary until chicken is cooked through.

Place skewers on a platter with sauce bowl and serve.

Nutritional Data

PER SERVING		EXCHANGES	
Calories	155	Milk	0.0
% Calories from fat	30	Veg.	0.0
Fat (gm)	5.1	Fruit	0.0
Sat. Fat (gm)	1.8	Bread	0.5
Cholesterol (mg)	46	Meat	2.0
Sodium (mg)	247	Fat	0.0
Protein (gm)	19		
Carbohydrate (gm)	7.6		

TURKEY SAUSAGE WITH SWEET PEPPERS

Makes 8 servings

Olive-oil-flavored non-stick cooking spray
4 smoked turkey sausages, about 2 ozs. each,
   room temperature
1 cup sliced onion
2 cups sliced red or green bell peppers
1 cup sliced tomatoes
½ teaspoon fennel seeds
1 teaspoon chopped oregano, or ½ teaspoon
   dried
¼ teaspoon garlic powder

S pray a grill rack and place it on grid over ashen-hot coals. Grill sausages, onions, peppers, and tomatoes, turning as necessary until done. It will take longer to cook the sausages than the vegetables, so start with the sausages and add the vegetables as the sausage is cooking.

Remove food to a board. Cut sausages into small coin-shaped slices. Toss sausage with vegetables and seasonings.

Spoon onto individual dishes, and serve hot with Italian bread.

Nutritional Data

PER SERVING		EXCHANGES	
Calories	73	Milk	0.0
% Calories from fat	27	Veg.	1.0
Fat (gm)	2.3	Fruit	0.0
Sat. Fat (gm)	0.6	Bread	0.0
Cholesterol (mg)	18	Meat	1.0
Sodium (mg)	243	Fat	0.0
Protein (gm)	6		
Carbohydrate (gm)	7.8		

SOFT-SHELL CRABS WITH YOGURT CHILI SAUCE

The soft-shell crab season is from spring through summer. To clean soft-shell crabs, remove the face section of the crab. Lift the shell on both sides of the back, then with a small, sharp knife scrape off the gills. Remove the sand. It is best to ask your fishmonger to clean the crabs for you.

Makes 8 servings

Yogurt Chili Sauce

- 2 cups plain non-fat yogurt
- ¼ cup chili sauce
- ¼ cup minced onion
- ½ teaspoon chili powder

Soft-Shell Crabs

- 1 cup flavored breadcrumbs
- 1 teaspoon marjoram, *or* ¼ teaspoon dried
- 2 tablespoons minced parsley
- ¼ teaspoon pepper
- 2 egg whites, slightly beaten
- 8 soft-shell crabs, cleaned, washed, patted dry with paper toweling
  Non-stick cooking spray

Yogurt Chili Sauce: Combine all ingredients in a small bowl. Cover and refrigerate until ready to serve. Stir and taste to adjust seasoning.

Soft-Shell Crabs: Mix together breadcrumbs, marjoram, parsley, and pepper. Spread crumbs on a flat dish.

Put slightly beaten egg whites in a separate shallow bowl.

When ready to grill, roll the crabs in the egg whites and dust with breadcrumb mixture.

Spray a grill rack and adjust it on the grid over ashen-hot coals. Grill crabs 3 to 4 minutes on each side or until crabs change from a bluish color to a reddish hue. They will be slightly firm to the touch.

Serve one crab per person and pass the chili sauce.

Nutritional Data

PER SERVING		EXCHANGES	
Calories	125	Milk	0.0
% Calories from fat	7	Veg.	0.0
Fat (gm)	0.9	Fruit	0.0
Sat. Fat (gm)	0.2	Bread	1.0
Cholesterol (mg)	13.6	Meat	1.0
Sodium (mg)	812	Fat	0.0
Protein (gm)	11.2		
Carbohydrate (gm)	17.5		

TURKEY MINI-BURGERS

As an alternative, you can serve these mini-burgers with cranberry relish.

Makes 8 servings

Burgers

- 1 lb. ground turkey breast meat
- 2 egg whites
- ¼ cup finely ground whole-wheat breadcrumbs
- ¾ cup minced onion
- 2 tablespoons chopped drained capers
- ¼ teaspoon pepper

Accompaniments

- 2 thin slices rye or pumpernickel bread, cut into 8 triangles
  Lettuce leaves, cut to bread size
- 8 thin slices tomato
- 1 medium-small red onion, cut into thin slices

Burgers: In a mixing bowl, combine ground turkey with egg whites, crumbs, onions, capers, and peppers.

Shape into 8 small burgers. Place burgers on a plate and refrigerate until ready to grill.

Spray grill rack and adjust it on grid over ashen-hot coals. Grill burgers 1 minute on each side, and continue cooking until turkey is cooked through but not overcooked. Remove turkey burgers with a long-handled spatula.

Accompaniments: Place lettuce leaves on bread and top with a tomato slices. Add burgers and finish with onion rings. Serve hot.

Nutritional Data

PER SERVING		EXCHANGES	
Calories	103	Milk	0.0
% Calories from fat	14	Veg.	0.0
Fat (gm)	1.6	Fruit	0.0
Sat. Fat (gm)	0.4	Bread	0.5
Cholesterol (mg)	25	Meat	1.5
Sodium (mg)	126	Fat	0.0
Protein (gm)	13		
Carbohydrate (gm)	9		

GRILLED PORTOBELLO MUSHROOMS

Use the stems of the mushrooms, chopped, in a salad or in a soup.

Makes 4 servings

Marinade
- 1 cup balsamic vinegar, *or* red wine vinegar
- ½ cup water, *or* vegetable stock
- ½ cup chopped onion
- 1 lemon, sliced
- 2 bay leaves
- 1 teaspoon fresh oregano, *or* ½ teaspoon dried
- 1 teaspoon fresh basil, *or* ½ teaspoon dried

Mushrooms
- 4 Portobello mushrooms, about 1 lb.
- Non-stick cooking spray

F irst prepare the marinade. Mix all marinade ingredients in a shallow bowl. Clean mushrooms and remove stems. (Chop and reserve stems for salad or a stuffed mushroom dish.) Put mushrooms in marinade and let stand for 1 hour. Turn mushrooms once or twice. Drain.

Spray grill rack and place it on grid over ashen-hot coals. Grill mushrooms about 2 minutes on each side.

Remove mushrooms, cut into strips, and serve a few slices on individual plates garnished with grilled green onions and/or cherry tomatoes.

Nutritional Data

PER SERVING		EXCHANGES	
Calories	56	Milk	0.0
% Calories from fat	26	Veg.	2.0
Fat (gm)	2.1	Fruit	0.0
Sat. Fat (gm)	0	Bread	0.0
Cholesterol (mg)	0	Meat	0.0
Sodium (mg)	8.6	Fat	0.0
Protein (gm)	3.9		
Carbohydrate (gm)	9.5		

3.
VEGETABLES

Grilled Vegetables with Pasta

Vegetables Grilled à la South of France

Grilled Vegetables on Warm Focaccia

String Beans and Asparagus with Pesto Dipping Sauce

Grilled Sweet Peppers Salad

Grilled Eggplant Spread

Vegetables and Potatoes with Pasta

Double-Baked Potatoes with Chili Sauce

Baked Potatoes with Garlic and Mustard Topping

Vegetable Kabobs with Sweet Potatoes and Bananas

Eggplant Steaks with Sour Cream and Wasabi

Vegetable Tortillas

Veggie Pizza on the Grill

GRILLED VEGETABLES WITH PASTA

Grilled vegetables are a treat. A simple recipe for grilled vegetables is to slice and cook them on a sprayed grill rack only until just done. Arrange the vegetables on a platter, and sprinkle them with balsamic vinegar.

Makes 4 entree servings

1 zucchini, cut in ¼-in. diagonal slices

4 summer squash, cut in half

1 large red or green bell pepper, seeded from the top, cut in round slices

1 red onion, sliced
Non-stick cooking spray

⅓ cup balsamic vinegar

12 ozs. penne, *or* pasta of your choice, cooked according to pkg. directions

½ cup non-fat ricotta cheese

½ cup plain non-fat yogurt

1 tablespoon basil

2 teaspoons chopped chives

½ teaspoon garlic powder

¼ teaspoon each ingredient: salt and pepper

2 tablespoons fresh-grated Parmesan cheese

C ut vegetables and have them ready by the grill.
Spray a grill rack and place it on the grid over hot or ashen coals. Grill vegetables a few minutes on each side until tender. Vegetables will char slightly. The vegetables will grill at different speeds, so remove them as they are ready. Sprinkle vegetables with balsamic vinegar.

Put hot drained pasta in a deep glass bowl. Toss pasta with vegetables and remaining ingredients. Best served hot.

Nutritional Data

PER SERVING		EXCHANGES	
Calories	400	Milk	0.0
% Calories from fat	8	Veg.	2.0
Fat (gm)	3.7	Fruit	0.0
Sat. Fat (gm)	1	Bread	4.0
Cholesterol (mg)	6	Meat	1.0
Sodium (mg)	248	Fat	0.0
Protein (gm)	20.1		
Carbohydrate (gm)	72.8		

VEGETABLES GRILLED À LA SOUTH OF FRANCE

Ratatouille has become a fall favorite recipe. That is when the vegetables are at their peak. To prepare this dish, the vegetables are grilled and served together in a medley, capturing the flavor of a ratatouille. Vegetables grill well over ashen rather than hot coals.

Makes 4 servings

1 small eggplant, peeled, sliced
1 medium zucchini, sliced
1 large tomato, sliced
1 green bell pepper, seeded, sliced
1 cup sliced onion
  Non-stick cooking spray
1 tablespoon chopped basil
2 teaspoons olive oil
½ teaspoon oregano
¼ teaspoon each ingredient: salt, and pepper

O ver a double thickness of paper towels, sprinkle eggplant with salt. Let stand 30 minutes. Wash salt off eggplant. Slice remaining vegetables and place near grill.

Spray grill rack and position it on grid over hot or ashen coals. Place eggplant on rack first, as it takes longer to cook, 10 to 20 minutes, depending on heat of coals and distance from them. Add remaining vegetables. Grill vegetables about 2 minutes per side, turning them as necessary with a long-handled spatula and fork. Vegetables will char slightly and should be hot. Put vegetables on a large serving plate.

Sprinkle vegetables with basil, olive oil, oregano, salt and pepper. Good hot or cold.

Nutritional Data

PER SERVING		EXCHANGES	
Calories	76	Milk	0.0
% Calories from fat	29	Veg.	2.0
Fat (gm)	2.7	Fruit	0.0
Sat. Fat (gm)	0.4	Bread	0.0
Cholesterol (mg)	0	Meat	0.0
Sodium (mg)	141	Fat	0.5
Protein (gm)	2.1		
Carbohydrate (gm)	12.8		

GRILLED VEGETABLES ON WARM FOCACCIA

Focaccia comes ready made at the grocery stores. If you want to prepare your own, the next recipe will guide you. Either way, enjoy your grilled vegetables on warm focaccia.

Makes 6 entree servings

Whole-Wheat Focaccia (recipe follows)
- ½ cup dried oregano, soaked in water 5 minutes, drained
- ½ medium eggplant, trimmed, peeled, sliced thin
- 1 lb. thin asparagus, trimmed
- 1 large tomato, sliced
- 4 cloves elephant garlic, peeled, sliced lengthwise
- 1 large onion, peeled, sliced
  Non-stick cooking spray
- ½ cup Italian parsley, chopped
- ⅓ cup red wine vinegar
- 1 tablespoon oregano

Sprinkle drained oregano over the hot coals as an aromatic for the vegetables. Cut and trim vegetables and have them handy near the grill. Spray a grill rack and place it on the grid over hot or ashen coals.

Spray vegetables lightly, and place eggplant on the grill rack first, as it will take the longest to cook. Add remaining vegetables and grill on both sides until vegetables are just tender. Vegetables will char slightly. Turn vegetables as necessary as they grill.

Remove vegetables to a platter. Sprinkle with parsley, vinegar, and ground oregano.

Spread the vegetables on one of the focaccias. Cover with the other focaccia, and cut into 6 servings. Best served hot.

Whole-Wheat Focaccia

Makes 6 servings, two 9-in. rounds

- ½ teaspoon honey
- 1 cup (scant) warm water
- 1 pkg. active dry yeast
- ¾ cup whole-wheat flour
- 2 cups all-purpose flour

½ cup white cornmeal
½ teaspoon salt
1 tablespoon olive oil
  Non-stick cooking spray

Stir honey into the warm water in a measuring cup or small bowl. Sprinkle yeast over water and stir until yeast dissolves. Let mixture stand in draft-free area about 5 minutes or until yeast begins to bubble.

Mix flour and cornmeal with salt and oil in a food processor fitted with a steel blade or in an electric mixer with a dough hook. To mix dough by hand, use a bowl and wooden spoon.

Pour in yeast mixture and process until a soft, almost sticky dough is formed, 5 to 10 seconds. If using an electric mixer, mix 3 minutes or until a smooth dough is formed. If mixing dough by hand, mix ingredients until a smooth, slightly sticky dough is formed, 3 to 5 minutes.

Knead dough by hand on a lightly floured board or pastry cloth until smooth. If dough is too sticky, add flour by the tablespoon until it reaches the desired consistency. Put dough in a bowl and cover lightly with oiled plastic wrap and aluminum foil or a kitchen towel.

Let dough rise until it doubles in bulk, 45 minutes to 1 hour. Punch dough down and let stand 5 minutes. Knead for a few minutes more on a lightly floured board or pastry cloth.

Divide dough in half and pat each half into a sprayed 9-inch baking pan or spring-form pan. Preheat oven to 375°. Bake focaccia in the center of the oven for 25 minute or until it tests done. The focaccia is done when a toothpick inserted in the center comes out dry. It will be a golden brown on top and firm to the touch. Remove from the oven and cool.

Nutritional Data

PER SERVING		EXCHANGES	
Calories	317	Milk	0.0
% Calories from fat	10	Veg.	2.0
Fat (gm)	3.8	Fruit	0.0
Sat. Fat (gm)	0.6	Bread	3.5
Cholesterol (mg)	0	Meat	0.0
Sodium (mg)	193	Fat	0.5
Protein (gm)	10.1		
Carbohydrate (gm)	63.1		

STRING BEANS AND ASPARAGUS WITH PESTO DIPPING SAUCE

The vegetables that you use can vary according to what is available at the market or your individual taste. String beans happen to be one of my very favorite vegetables, so you may see them in many of the recipes. The vegetables are served on individual plates, and each guest has a small bowl of dipping sauce.

Makes 4 entree servings

Pesto Dipping Sauce

- 2 cups, firmly packed, fresh red or green basil leaves
- 3 cloves garlic
- ¼ cup fresh-grated Parmesan cheese
- ½ cup vegetable stock
- 2 tablespoons pine nuts
- 1 tablespoon olive oil

Vegetables

- ½ lb. string beans, trimmed, whole, blanched
- ½ lb. thin asparagus, trimmed, whole, blanched
  Non-stick cooking spray
- ½ cup tarragon, for aroma, optional, soaked in water 5 minutes, drained
- 1 tablespoon ground tarragon
- 3 cups cooked no-egg noodles, *or* rice

Pesto Dipping Sauce: Use a food processor fitted with steel blade. Add basil, garlic, cheese, and stock; process until pureed. Add pine nuts and again process briefly. In a slow, steady stream, add olive oil through the feed tube.

Spoon the pesto into 4 sauce dishes. Cover and refrigerate until ready to serve. Stir the pesto before serving.

Vegetables: Trim the vegetables and have them near the grill. Spray grill rack. Sprinkle drained tarragon over ashen-hot coals. Set rack on grid over hot coals. Spray vegetables lightly, sprinkle with ground tarragon, and place them on rack. Grill vegetables about 2 minutes per side or until tender, turning them as necessary using a long-handled spatula and fork. Vegetables will char slightly and should be hot and crisp.

Divide the vegetables, and present them on individual plates. Bring to the table along with individual sauce dishes of dipping sauce. Serve with rice.

Nutritional Data

PER SERVING		EXCHANGES	
Calories	276	Milk	0.0
% Calories from fat	30	Veg.	1.5
Fat (gm)	9.7	Fruit	0.0
Sat. Fat (gm)	1.9	Bread	2.0
Cholesterol (mg)	4.9	Meat	0.5
Sodium (mg)	170	Fat	1.5
Protein (gm)	13.5		
Carbohydrate (gm)	37.8		

GRILLED SWEET PEPPERS SALAD

You can use all one color bell peppers or vary them as is done in this recipe.

Makes 4 servings

Non-stick cooking spray
2 red bell peppers, whole
1 green bell pepper, whole
1 yellow bell pepper, whole
1 clove elephant garlic, peeled, sliced lengthwise
1 teaspoon olive oil
1 tablespoon balsamic vinegar
¼ teaspoon each ingredient: salt, pepper, and
   oregano

Spray grill rack. Place rack on grid over hot or ashen coals. Place peppers and garlic on rack. Grill about 9 minutes, turning peppers about every 3 minutes as they char. Remove peppers and garlic from grill, and transfer garlic to a plate.

Place peppers in plastic bag and seal securely. Let peppers stand 12 minutes. Using a paper towel, rub off the charred skins of the peppers. Remove the seeds. Cut peppers into strips.

Sprinkle with the grilled garlic, olive oil, vinegar, salt, pepper, and oregano.

Nutritional Data

PER SERVING		EXCHANGES	
Calories	37	Milk	0.0
% Calories from fat	29	Veg.	1.5
Fat (gm)	1.3	Fruit	0.0
Sat. Fat (gm)	0.2	Bread	0.0
Cholesterol (mg)	0	Meat	0.0
Sodium (mg)	136	Fat	0.0
Protein (gm)	0.8		
Carbohydrate (gm)	6.3		

GRILLED EGGPLANT SPREAD

It is the slightly smoky flavor of the grilled eggplant that gives this spread its unique taste.

Makes 6 servings

- 2 medium-large eggplants, peeled, sliced
  Non-stick cooking spray
- 3 tablespoons fresh lemon juice
- 1 tablespoon olive oil
- ½ teaspoon powdered garlic
- ⅓ cup non-fat ricotta cheese
- ¼ cup plain non-fat yogurt
- ¼ teaspoon each ingredient: salt, pepper, and cumin seeds
- ¼ cup minced parsley, *or* cilantro

Peel and slice eggplants. Over a double thickness of paper towels or in a colander, sprinkle eggplant with salt. Let stand 30 minutes, then wash salt off eggplant. Place eggplant on a plate near the grill.

Spray a grill rack. Set rack on grid over hot or ashen coals. Place eggplant on rack and grill, turning as necessary, until it is soft and cooked to taste.

Puree eggplant in food processor fitted with steel blade or use blender. Add lemon juice, oil, garlic powder, ricotta cheese, yogurt, salt, pepper, cumin seeds, and parsley. Mix to combine.

Spoon eggplant spread into a serving bowl and cover. Refrigerate spread until serving time. Stir before serving and adjust seasonings to taste.

Nutritional Data

PER SERVING		EXCHANGES	
Calories	73	Milk	0.0
% Calories from fat	29	Veg.	2.0
Fat (gm)	2.6	Fruit	0.0
Sat. Fat (gm)	0.4	Bread	0.0
Cholesterol (mg)	1.5	Meat	0.0
Sodium (mg)	108	Fat	0.5
Protein (gm)	3.5		
Carbohydrate (gm)	10.8		

VEGETABLES AND POTATOES WITH PASTA

These grilled vegetables can be served alone or tossed with cooked pasta of your choice. The recipe can easily be doubled, and the vegetables can be varied. Potatoes grill well and taste so good prepared over the coals.

Makes 4 entree servings

Pasta Sauce

- Non-stick cooking spray
- 1 cup chopped onion
- 2 cloves garlic, minced
- ½ cup shredded carrots
- 1 can (16 ozs.) crushed tomatoes, include juice
- 1 teaspoon tarragon
- ½ teaspoon rosemary
- ¼ teaspoon each ingredient: salt and pepper

Vegetables and Pasta

- 1 small eggplant, peeled
- 2 boiling potatoes, about 5 ozs. each, skin on, scrubbed, parboiled until fork tender
- 1 bunch green onions, trimmed
- 2 tomatoes, chopped
- 2 cups whole-wheat spaghetti, *or* pasta of your choice, cooked according to pkg. directions, drained, run under hot water to refresh before serving

Pasta Sauce: Can be made the day before serving for convenience. Heat a sprayed non-stick saucepan. Sauté onions, garlic, and carrots, covered, over medium heat 4 to 5 minutes or until onions are tender. Stir occasionally. Mix in tomatoes, including juice, tarragon, rosemary, salt, and pepper. Simmer sauce 5 minutes, stirring occasionally. Set sauce aside. Reheat to serve.

Vegetables and Pasta: Over a double thickness of paper towels or in a colander, sprinkle eggplant with salt. Let stand 30 minutes. Wash salt off eggplant, slice, and transfer to a plate near grill. When potatoes are cool enough to handle, cut them into thin slices.

Spray grill rack. Set rack on grid over hot coals. Place eggplant on rack first, as it needs 10 to 20 minutes to grill, turning as necessary. Add potatoes and onions, grilling them 2 to 4 minutes per side. Brush all vegetables with the sauce when you turn them. Add tomatoes and grill on one side only until tomato is hot, about 1 minute.

Toss all vegetables, except green onions, with remaining sauce and hot, drained pasta. Serve on individual plates with green onions sprinkled on top.

Nutritional Data

PER SERVING		EXCHANGES	
Calories	231	Milk	0.0
% Calories from fat	5	Veg.	2.0
Fat (gm)	1.3	Fruit	0.0
Sat. Fat (gm)	0.2	Bread	2.5
Cholesterol (mg)	0	Meat	0.0
Sodium (mg)	338	Fat	0.0
Protein (gm)	8.2		
Carbohydrate (gm)	51.5		

DOUBLE-BAKED POTATOES WITH CHILI SAUCE

In the grilling technique, you position the food on a grill rack about 5 to 6 inches above the hot coals. This dry heat method allows the food to take on the smoky flavors of the charcoal. For best results, always use hardwood charcoal along with aromatic wood chips and/or dry herbs.

Makes 8 servings

4 baked potatoes, 5–6 ozs. each, skin on, scrubbed
Aluminum foil, heavy-duty

Chili Sauce

1 cup plain non-fat yogurt
1 can (4 ozs.) chopped green, mild or hot chilies, drained
1 teaspoon dried onion flakes
½ teaspoon each ingredient: ground cumin and garlic powder

S crub potatoes under cold running water. Dry and wrap each potato individually in heavy-duty aluminum foil.

When coals are hot, place potatoes directly on hot coals around perimeter of grill. If you are grilling other food at this time, replace grid and rack and continue cooking.

Potatoes should be turned every 10 minutes until done. Potatoes are cooked when they are easily pierced with the tip of a knife, 35 to 40 minutes, depending on size of potatoes, heat, and outdoor temperature.

Chili Sauce: Prepare the sauce while potatoes are cooking. Put yogurt in a glass bowl and mix in remaining ingredients. Cover and refrigerate until serving time.

Carefully remove potatoes from grill to kitchen counter, using a long-handled spoon and pot holders. Remove and discard foil. When potatoes have cooled enough to handle, cut them in halves lengthwise. Scoop out soft flesh, leaving skin intact with small lining of potato. Mash the hot potato flesh, and mix in ¼ cup of sauce. Mound the mashed potatoes back into potato skins. Put potatoes back on the grill, cover, and cook 5 minutes or until potatoes are hot.

Present potatoes on individual plates. Spoon remaining sauce over them and serve immediately.

Nutritional Data

PER SERVING		EXCHANGES	
Calories	91	Milk	0.0
% Calories from fat	2	Veg.	0.0
Fat (gm)	0.2	Fruit	0.0
Sat. Fat (gm)	0.1	Bread	1.5
Cholesterol (mg)	1	Meat	0.0
Sodium (mg)	193	Fat	0.0
Protein (gm)	3.3		
Carbohydrate (gm)	19.8		

BAKED POTATOES WITH GARLIC AND MUSTARD TOPPING

This method of cooking directly on the coals is really campfire cooking, or "ember" cooking. Grilled garlic takes on a less pungent taste, and it is easy to squeeze out of the skin, which is then discarded.

Makes 8 servings

- 4 baking potatoes, 5–6 ozs. each, skin on, scrubbed
- 8 cloves elephant garlic, skin intact
  Aluminum foil, heavy-duty

Mustard Topping
- 1 cup plain non-fat yogurt
- 2 tablespoons fat-free mayonnaise
- 1 tablespoon Dijon-style mustard, or to taste
- 1 tablespoon chopped parsley
- ¼ teaspoon freshly ground black pepper

Scrub potatoes under cold running water. Dry and wrap each potato individually in heavy-duty aluminum foil.

When coals are hot, place potatoes directly on hot coals around perimeter of grill. If you are grilling other food at this time, replace grid and rack and continue cooking.

Potatoes should be turned every 10 minutes until done. Potatoes are cooked when they are easily pierced with the tip of a knife, 35 to 40 minutes, depending on size of potatoes, heat, and outdoor temperature.

About 10 minutes before estimated finish time of potatoes, place cloves of garlic on the grill. Turn garlic every 3 to 6 minutes until it can easily be pierced with the tip of a knife and is soft.

Mustard Topping: While vegetables are cooking, prepare the topping. Put yogurt and mayonnaise in a small glass bowl. Mix in mustard, parsley, and pepper. Cover and refrigerate until serving time.

Using pot holders, remove potatoes and garlic from grill to serving plate. Discard foil and cut potatoes in halves lengthwise. Place a garlic clove next to each potato half. Instruct guests to squeeze out garlic and spread it over the potato. Pass topping at the table.

Nutritional Data

PER SERVING		EXCHANGES	
Calories	96	Milk	0.0
% Calories from fat	2	Veg.	0.0
Fat (gm)	0.3	Fruit	0.0
Sat. Fat (gm)	0.1	Bread	1.5
Cholesterol (mg)	1	Meat	0.0
Sodium (mg)	100	Fat	0.0
Protein (gm)	3.4		
Carbohydrate (gm)	20.5		

Vegetable Kabobs with Sweet Potatoes and Bananas

The potato is partially cooked before threading onto the skewers. If you are using bamboo skewers, soak them in water for 15 minutes before using. This soaking procedure is done so that the bamboo skewers will not char during cooking. Another choice to help prevent charring is to wrap the ends of the skewers in aluminum foil before grilling.

Makes 4 servings

Cilantro Brushing Sauce
- 2 teaspoons diet margarine, melted
- ⅓ cup minced cilantro, *or* parsley
- ¼ teaspoon each ingredient: ground cumin, salt, and pepper

Vegetables and Fruit
- 4 short skewers, *or* double-pronged skewers
- 2 bananas, peeled, cut into 1½–2-in. pieces
- 3 tablespoons fresh lemon juice, *or* lime juice
- 2 sweet potatoes, about 6 ozs. each, peeled, parboiled until fork tender, drained, and cut into 1-in. pieces
- 4 medium-hot peppers, seeded carefully, cut into 1½-in. squares
- 16 cherry tomatoes, washed, stems removed, cut into halves
- Non-stick cooking spray

Cilantro Brushing Sauce: To prepare sauce, put melted margarine in a bowl. Mix in remaining ingredients. Set aside.

Vegetables and Fruit: Sprinkle bananas with juice.

Thread skewers, alternating sweet potatoes, peppers, tomatoes, and bananas.

Spray a grill rack and position it on grid over hot coals. Place kabobs on grill rack. Grill kabobs, turning them as the vegetables begin to char. Grill about 2 minutes on each side. Rotate so that all sides of the kabobs are cooked. Kabobs are done when vegetables are hot and slightly charred. Serve hot.

Nutritional Data

PER SERVING		EXCHANGES	
Calories	157	Milk	0.0
% Calories from fat	9	Veg.	1.0
Fat (gm)	1.7	Fruit	1.0
Sat. Fat (gm)	0.3	Bread	1.0
Cholesterol (mg)	0	Meat	0.0
Sodium (mg)	172	Fat	0.0
Protein (gm)	2.9		
Carbohydrate (gm)	35.8		

EGGPLANT STEAKS WITH SOUR CREAM AND WASABI

Carolyn Collins of the caviar company that bears her name suggested grilling an eggplant steak, spreading it with sour cream while the eggplant was still hot, and adding a sprinkle of Wasabi Tobikko, a Japanese product consisting of flying fish roe flavored with neon green wasabi, the oriental horseradish. Wasabi Tobikko is available from Collins Caviar, 925 W. Jackson Blvd., Chicago, IL 60607, (312)226-0342.

Makes 6 servings

- 1 medium-large eggplant, a short, round eggplant preferable
- 1 slice day-old whole-wheat bread, made into crumbs
- ¼ teaspoon each ingredient: pepper and rosemary
  Non-stick cooking spray
- 1½ cups non-fat sour cream
- 1 tablespoon Wasabi Tobikko, *or* regular wasabi

P eel and slice eggplant. Over a double thickness of paper towels or in a colander, sprinkle eggplant with salt. Let stand 30 minutes, then wash salt off eggplant. Pat eggplant dry using paper towels. Position eggplant on a plate near the grill.

In a small bowl, mix breadcrumbs with pepper and rosemary. Pat crumbs onto eggplant.

Spray a grill rack. Set rack on grid over ashen coals. Place eggplant on rack. Grill eggplant steaks, turning as necessary until soft, 15 to 20 minutes altogether.

Place a slice of eggplant on individual plates. Spread sour cream on top and sprinkle center of eggplant with Wasabi Tobikko. Serve hot.

Nutritional Data

PER SERVING		EXCHANGES	
Calories	65	Milk	0.0
% Calories from fat	5	Veg.	1.0
Fat (gm)	0.4	Fruit	0.0
Sat. Fat (gm)	0.1	Bread	0.5
Cholesterol (mg)	7	Meat	0.0
Sodium (mg)	63	Fat	0.0
Protein (gm)	5.1		
Carbohydrate (gm)	11.9		

VEGETABLE TORTILLAS

Vegetables can be grilled over hot or ashen coals. Naturally, if you are using ashen coals, it will take longer than if you are using hot coals. If you are using hot coals, watch the vegetables closely so they do not overcook.

Makes 4 servings

Mopping Sauce
- ¼ cup fresh lime juice
- ¼ cup fresh lemon juice
- 2 tablespoons dark molasses
- 2 tablespoons ketchup
- 1 tablespoon canola oil
- ½ teaspoon garlic powder
- ¼ teaspoon cumin seeds

Vegetables
- 1 cup thinly sliced red onion
- 2 tomatoes, sliced
- 1 green bell pepper, seeded, sliced
- 1 red bell pepper, seeded, sliced thin
- 1 cup sliced zucchini
- 1 cup yellow squash, sliced thin
- 1 teaspoon chili powder
- ½ teaspoon cumin seeds
- 2 jalapeño peppers, seeded carefully, chopped
  Non-stick cooking spray
- 4 corn tortillas, warmed on the grill just before serving

Mopping Sauce: Combine all ingredients in a glass bowl.
Vegetables: Cut up and place them near grill.

Spray grill rack and place it on grid over ashen-hot coals. It might be necessary to grill the vegetables in two batches. Put half of the vegetables on the rack, mop them liberally with sauce, and continue mopping when you turn them. Vegetables will grill at different rates of from 1 (tomatoes) to 4 (squash) minutes; turn as necessary. Remove vegetables to a plate as they become warm and tender.

Sprinkle vegetables with chili powder, cumin seeds, and hot peppers. Spoon vegetables into center of each warm tortilla. Roll up tortillas and serve.

Nutritional Data

PER SERVING		EXCHANGES	
Calories	178	Milk	0.0
% Calories from fat	22	Veg.	4.0
Fat (gm)	4.7	Fruit	0.0
Sat. Fat (gm)	0.4	Bread	0.5
Cholesterol (mg)	0	Meat	0.0
Sodium (mg)	168	Fat	1.0
Protein (gm)	3.9		
Carbohydrate (gm)	34.1		

VEGGIE PIZZA ON THE GRILL

The directions for a homemade crust are given, but if time is short, use a prepared crust, a boboli, or even French bread rolls sliced lengthwise. Of course, the nutritional values will change if you depart from the recipe.

Makes 6 servings

Herb Crust

- 1 teaspoon active dry yeast
- 1½ cups all-purpose flour
- ¼ teaspoon salt
- 1 teaspoon olive oil
- 1 teaspoon each ingredient: rosemary and sage
- ½ cup warm water
  Non-stick cooking spray

Topping

- 2 green bell peppers, seeded, sliced round
- 1 lb. mushrooms, trimmed, sliced
- 1 tomato, sliced
- 1 cup sliced onion
- 1 teaspoon oregano
- ½ teaspoon garlic powder
- ⅓ cup skim mozzarella cheese

Herb Crust: Combine all ingredients in an electric mixer or food processor. Mix until dough is smooth. If dough is too sticky, sprinkle with a few tablespoons of flour. Remove dough and place it in ceramic or glass bowl. Cover with an oiled sheet of wax paper. Locate bowl in a dry, warm area so dough can rise 45 minutes to 1 hour. Punch dough down and let stand 10 minutes.

Spray a 12-inch pizza pan. Press dough into pan, shaping a rim as you press it evenly around edge. Preheat oven to 425°. Bake crust in center of oven for 8 minutes or until it begins to color. Dough should be firm. Crust can be prepared ahead of time.

Topping: Spray a grill rack. Set rack on grid over ashen coals. Grill vegetables, turning as needed. The peppers will take longest to grill, so put them on first. Grilling time is 5 to 8 minutes.

To assemble, decoratively arrange vegetables on pizza crust. Sprinkle with oregano, garlic powder, and cheese. Slide pizza onto grill over preheated tiles or grill rack. Cover grill and cook only until warm and crisp, 3 to 4 minutes, depending on heat of coals.

Remove cooked pizza carefully from the grill, using a pizza paddle or large spatula. Cut into slices and serve.

Nutritional Data

PER SERVING		EXCHANGES	
Calories	197	Milk	0.0
% Calories from fat	16	Veg.	2.5
Fat (gm)	3.6	Fruit	0.0
Sat. Fat (gm)	1.5	Bread	1.5
Cholesterol (mg)	7	Meat	0.0
Sodium (mg)	155	Fat	0.5
Protein (gm)	8.9		
Carbohydrate (gm)	33.3		

4.
SEAFOOD

Mahimahi in Corn Husks with Corn Relish

Teriyaki Salmon Fillets with Grilled Mushrooms

Salmon Burgers

Sole Grilled on Orange Slices with Orange-Mustard Sauce

Striped Bass with Potato-Zucchini Salad

Sweet-and-Sour Shark Steaks on Buckwheat Noodles

Tuna with Capers and Tarragon

Marinated Bluefish with Grilled Tomatoes

Grouper *au Poivre* with Basil Sauce

Scrod with Fennel

Halibut with Peach Chutney

Grilled Seafood Paella

Smoky Scallops and Wilted Spinach Salad

Mahimahi in Corn Husks with Corn Relish

This recipe makes a very interesting party presentation. The rule of thumb for grilling fish is 10 minutes per inch of thickness of the fish. Black sea bass or halibut is an acceptable substitution for this medium-textured fish with a delicate flavor.

Makes 4 servings

Corn Relish

- 1 teaspoon canola oil
- 2 cups fresh corn kernels
- 1 green or red bell pepper, seeded, chopped
- ½ cup chopped celery
- ½ cup chopped onion
- ¼ cup white vinegar
- 3 tablespoons sugar
- ½ teaspoon each ingredient: celery seeds and turmeric
- ¼ teaspoon salt

Mahimahi

- Corn husks from 4 ears of corn, discard silk, soak in water 30 minutes, and drain
- 1¼ lbs. mahimahi fillets, cut into 4 portions
- 4 teaspoons canola oil
- ½ cup chopped cilantro

- 3–4 4-in. pieces of mesquite wood, soaked in water 30 minutes, drained
- Non-stick cooking spray

Corn Relish: Prepare the day before serving. Heat oil in a non-stick saucepan over medium heat. Sauté corn 2 minutes. Add pepper, celery, onions, vinegar, sugar, celery seeds, turmeric, and salt. Simmer 4 minutes. Spoon relish into a bowl and cool. Cover lightly and refrigerate until needed. Stir before serving.

Mahimahi: To wrap each fish fillet, first set out a husk on the counter. Put fillet in the husk, brush fish with oil, and sprinkle it with cilantro. Encase fish with corn husk, making it look as if the corn cob were back inside.

Arrange the drained mesquite wood over ashen-hot coal. Spray grid and grill fish in the husk about 8 minutes or until done to taste. Turn once with a long-handled spatula. When you think fish is cooked, remove one packet, open it, and test for doneness. Fish is done when it flakes easily when prodded with a fork.

Place one husk packet on each plate, and serve with corn relish.

Nutritional Data

PER SERVING		EXCHANGES	
Calories	297	Milk	0.0
% Calories from fat	21	Veg.	0.5
Fat (gm)	7	Fruit	0.0
Sat. Fat (gm)	0.7	Bread	2.0
Cholesterol (mg)	106	Meat	4.0
Sodium (mg)	282	Fat	0.0
Protein (gm)	30.2		
Carbohydrate (gm)	30.2		

TERIYAKI SALMON FILLETS WITH GRILLED MUSHROOMS

Shiitake are mushrooms that recently have been cultivated in the United States but grow wild in Japan. These mushrooms are sold both dried and fresh. If they are dried, they should be reconstituted in hot water for about 30 minutes and then drained.

Makes 4 servings

Teriyaki Brushing Sauce
- ⅓ cup low-sodium soy sauce
- 2 cloves garlic, minced
- ⅓ cup dry sherry
- ½ teaspoon powdered ginger
- ¼ teaspoon pepper

Salmon
- 4 5-oz. salmon fillets
- 8 large fresh or reconstituted shiitake mushrooms
- Non-stick cooking spray

Teriyaki Brushing Sauce: Combine soy sauce, garlic, sherry, ginger, and pepper in small glass bowl. Brush salmon fillets with sauce and let stand at room temperature 30 minutes. Clean mushrooms and trim stems; brush with sauce.

Salmon: Spray a grill rack and adjust it on grid over ashen-hot coals. Place salmon and mushrooms on rack. Cook mushrooms about 2 minutes; turn and cook another 1 to 2 minutes. Mushrooms will begin to char when ready. Grill salmon 3 to 4 minutes on each side; centers should be slightly translucent; do not overcook.

Serve fish with mushrooms and hot brown or white rice.

Nutritional Data

PER SERVING		EXCHANGES	
Calories	166	Milk	0.0
% Calories from fat	27	Veg.	1.0
Fat (gm)	4.9	Fruit	0.0
Sat. Fat (gm)	1	Bread	0.0
Cholesterol (mg)	25.4	Meat	2.5
Sodium (mg)	320	Fat	0.0
Protein (gm)	21.6		
Carbohydrate (gm)	6.6		

SALMON BURGERS

Salmon burgers can be prepared ahead of time and stored in the refrigerator. To freeze them, make the burgers, separate them with pieces of waxed paper or aluminum foil, place in a plastic bag, seal, and freeze.

Makes 4 servings

- 2 cups ground fresh salmon, *or* 1 can (16 ozs.) salmon, drained, bones discarded
- 1 egg white
- ½ cup whole-wheat breadcrumbs
- 1 tablespoon chopped dill
- ¼ teaspoon each ingredient: salt and pepper
  Non-stick cooking spray
- 4 hamburger rolls
- 4 teaspoons low-calorie mayonnaise
- 4 slices lettuce
- 4 slices tomato

Mash salmon in deep mixing bowl. Mix in egg white, breadcrumbs, dill, salt and pepper. Blend all ingredients. Shape salmon mixture into burgers, place on plate, and refrigerate until ready to grill.

Spray grill rack and place on grid over ashen-hot coals. Grill salmon burgers 1 minute on each side, and continue cooking until done to taste. Turn carefully with a long-handled spatula. Burgers will crust slightly.

Put the opened burger rolls on the grill rack to toast, being careful not to burn the bread.

To serve, spread mayonnaise on bottom of roll. Add lettuce and tomato slice, top with hot salmon burger, and serve.

Nutritional Data

PER SERVING		EXCHANGES	
Calories	300	Milk	0.0
% Calories from fat	26	Veg.	0.0
Fat (gm)	8.5	Fruit	0.0
Sat. Fat (gm)	1.8	Bread	2.0
Cholesterol (mg)	28	Meat	3.0
Sodium (mg)	553	Fat	0.0
Protein (gm)	22		
Carbohydrate (gm)	32.4		

SOLE GRILLED ON ORANGE SLICES WITH ORANGE-MUSTARD SAUCE

Sole is a light, delicate flat fish. So how can we grill it, you ask? Delicate food may be grilled successfully on a bed, or layer, of sliced fruit or vegetable. Not only does this allow you to grill the food but the fruit or vegetable slices impart a special flavor. In this recipe the thin sole is grilled on orange slices. If available, use blood oranges. They have a sweet yet somewhat tart flavor and a dark red, almost maroon color.

Makes 4 servings

Orange-Mustard Sauce
- 2 cups plain non-fat yogurt
- 2 tablespoons grated orange rind
- 2 tablespoons honey mustard
- 1 regular or blood orange, peeled, chopped

Sole
- Non-fat cooking spray
- ⅓ cup dried tarragon, rinsed, drained, for aromatic
- 2 regular or blood oranges, sliced thin
- 1½ lbs. sole fillets, cut into 4 portions

Orange-Mustard Sauce: Mix together all of the sauce ingredients in a small bowl. Lightly cover bowl and refrigerate until needed. Stir and taste sauce to adjust seasonings just before serving time.

Sole: Spray a grill rack. Sprinkle tarragon over ashen-hot coals, creating an aromatic flavoring for the fish. Set rack on grill grid. Arrange orange slices over grill rack to form a bed for the fish. Place sole fillets on the orange slices. Grill fish 3 to 6 minutes or until cooked; it will flake easily when prodded with a fork. Do not turn fish.

To serve, remove fish and orange slices with a long-handled spatula to individual dishes or a platter. Pass the orange-mustard sauce at the table. Regular or whole-wheat pasta or couscous make a good accompaniment.

Nutritional Data

PER SERVING		EXCHANGES	
Calories	257	Milk	0.5
% Calories from fat	9	Veg.	0.0
Fat (gm)	2.6	Fruit	1.0
Sat. Fat (gm)	0.7	Bread	0.0
Cholesterol (mg)	81.8	Meat	4.0
Sodium (mg)	311	Fat	0.0
Protein (gm)	36.3		
Carbohydrate (gm)	21.4		

STRIPED BASS WITH POTATO-ZUCCHINI SALAD

Striped bass is an Atlantic Coast fish that migrates from saltwater, where it lives, to fresh water to spawn. It is a firm-fleshed fish with mild flavor. Potato salad is a perfect accompaniment to most grilled foods. Here, we have made traditional potato salad lighter by the addition of vegetables, and we've used a reduced-fat mayonnaise in the dressing.

Makes 4 servings

3 handfuls of cut, dried grapevine (optional)
   Olive-oil-flavored non-stick cooking spray
2 lemons, sliced thin
4 small striped bass, 7–8 ozs. each, heads and
   tails intact
1 tablespoon minced garlic
¼ teaspoon pepper
2 tablespoons fresh oregano, *or* 2 teaspoons
   dried
   Potato-Zucchini Salad (recipe follows)

S oak grapevine 30 minutes and drain. Lightly spray fish and grill rack. Arrange lemon slices in fish cavities. Put the drained grapevines on ashen-hot coals, creating an aromatic flavoring for the fish. Place rack on the grill. Arrange fish on rack and sprinkle with garlic, pepper, and oregano.

Grill fish 5 to 6 minutes, then turn once with a long-handled spatula. Continue grilling about 3 minutes or until fish is cooked; it will flake easily when prodded with a fork.

Serve a whole fish on each plate with potato-zucchini salad.

Potato-Zucchini Salad
Makes 4 servings

1 lb. boiling potatoes
1 cup chopped onion

   1 cup thinly sliced zucchini
   ½ cup corn niblets
   ½ cup chopped celery

Light Dressing
   ½ cup low-calorie mayonnaise
   ½ cup plain non-fat yogurt
   2 tablespoons cider vinegar
   1 tablespoon sugar
   ½ teaspoon garlic powder
   ¼ teaspoon each ingredient: salt and pepper

Peel potatoes and cut into quarters. Slide potatoes into lightly salted boiling water in a large pot. Reduce heat and continue cooking over medium heat for 20 minutes or until potatoes are fork tender yet firm; do not let potatoes become mushy. Drain potatoes and cool. Cut potatoes into ½-inch cubes. Transfer potatoes to a glass bowl. Add onions, zucchini, corn, and celery.

Light Dressing: In a small bowl, combine all dressing ingredients. Toss potato salad with dressing. Taste to adjust seasonings.

This salad can be prepared the day before serving.

Nutritional Data

PER SERVING		EXCHANGES	
Calories	386	Milk	0.0
% Calories from fat	26	Veg.	2.0
Fat (gm)	11.3	Fruit	0.0
Sat. Fat (gm)	2.8	Bread	2.0
Cholesterol (mg)	59.3	Meat	3.0
Sodium (mg)	494	Fat	0.5
Protein (gm)	31.6		
Carbohydrate (gm)	40.6		

Sweet-and-Sour Shark Steaks on Buckwheat Noodles

Shark is a firm-fleshed fish well suited for the grill. Discard skin before grilling.

Makes 4 servings

Sweet-and-Sour Brushing Sauce
- 1 cup tomato juice
- ¼ cup red wine vinegar
- ¼ cup packed dark brown sugar
- 2 teaspoons honey mustard
- ⅓ cup chopped green onion
- ½ teaspoon garlic powder

Buckwheat Noodles
- 2 cups Japanese buckwheat noodles, cooked according to package directions, drained

Shark
- 4 shark steaks, about 6 ozs. each
- 4 green onions, trimmed

Sweet-and-Sour Brushing Sauce: Combine tomato juice, vinegar, sugar, mustard, onions, and garlic in a small saucepan. Simmer sauce for a few minutes, stirring often, just until ingredients are combined and hot. Cool.

Brush shark steaks with sauce. Put steaks on a plate and let stand 30 minutes.

Buckwheat Noodles: Cook noodles according to package directions. Drain and set aside.

Shark: Spray grill rack and adjust it on grid over ashen-hot coals. Place fish and green onions on rack. Cook onions 1 to 2 minutes, then turn and cook another 1 to 2 minutes. Onions will begin to char.

At the same time, grill fish about 4 minutes, turn, and continue grilling 2 to 3 minutes, depending on thickness of steaks. Fish is done when it flakes easily when prodded with tip of fork. Brush fish with sauce as it grills.

To serve, run noodles under hot water and drain. Divide noodles onto plates. Serve fish and green onions decoratively over the noodles. Pass extra brushing sauce at the table. Serve hot.

Nutritional Data

PER SERVING		EXCHANGES	
Calories	354	Milk	0.0
% Calories from fat	21	Veg.	0.0
Fat (gm)	8.3	Fruit	0.0
Sat. Fat (gm)	1.7	Bread	2.0
Cholesterol (mg)	86.1	Meat	4.0
Sodium (mg)	495	Fat	0.0
Protein (gm)	39.7		
Carbohydrate (gm)	30.2		

TUNA WITH CAPERS AND TARRAGON

Tuna is a firm fish with a high fat content. If tuna is not available, substitute swordfish in this recipe.

Makes 4 servings

Tarragon Marinade

¼ cup olive oil
¼ cup dry white wine
½ teaspoon garlic powder
3 tablespoons fresh minced tarragon, *or*
1½ teaspoons dried

Tuna

½ cup dried tarragon (optional) for aromatic
Non-stick cooking spray
4 5-oz. tuna fillets
1 tablespoon capers
4 teaspoons minced tarragon

Tarragon Marinade: Combine all ingredients in a small glass bowl. Drizzle and brush marinade over tuna. Place tuna and marinade in a plastic bag. Seal bag and turn it several times so that all sides of the tuna are covered by marinade. Place bag in refrigerator on a plate, and let fish marinate 2 to 3 hours. Drain before grilling.

Tuna: Soak tarragon 5 minutes and drain. Scatter tarragon over ashen-hot coals. Spray grill rack and place it on grid over hot coals. Grill tuna about 3 minutes on each side for medium-rare. Do not overcook fish or it will become tough.

Remove tuna to individual plates and sprinkle with capers and tarragon.

Nutritional Data

PER SERVING		EXCHANGES	
Calories	201	Milk	0.0
% Calories from fat	28	Veg.	0.0
Fat (gm)	6.1	Fruit	0.0
Sat. Fat (gm)	1.1	Bread	0.0
Cholesterol (mg)	67	Meat	4.0
Sodium (mg)	94	Fat	0.0
Protein (gm)	31.7		
Carbohydrate (gm)	2.3		

MARINATED BLUEFISH WITH GRILLED TOMATOES

Bluefish is a firm fish caught mostly off the coast of New England in the Atlantic. One summer we were walking along the shore in a Maine coastal town when we saw people running with buckets. The excitement was caused by bluefish. The hungry bluefish were chasing a school of mackerel onto the beach. The bluefish has a reputation of being a nasty fish with gluttonous tastes.

Makes 4 servings

Lemon and Thyme Marinade

¼ cup lemon juice

2 tablespoons fresh thyme, *or* 1 tablespoon dried

¼ teaspoon pepper

½ teaspoon garlic powder

Bluefish

Non-stick cooking spray

4 5-oz. bluefish fillets

2 large tomatoes, cut into thick ½-in. slices

Marinade: Combine all ingredients in a small glass bowl. Drizzle and brush marinade over bluefish fillets. Put bluefish and marinade in a plastic bag. Seal bag and turn it several times so that all sides of fish are covered with marinade. Put bag in refrigerator on a plate, and let fish marinate 2 to 3 hours. Drain fish before grilling.

Bluefish: Spray grill rack and position it on grid over ashen-hot coals. Grill the bluefish and tomato slices. Turn tomatoes once, using a long-handled spatula. Just warm the tomatoes; do not let them get mushy.

Grill bluefish 4 to 5 minutes, then turn it, using a long-handled spatula, and continue grilling about 2 minutes or until done to taste. The fish will flake when prodded with a fork when done. Be careful not to overcook. Remember that grilling time depends on thickness of fish, distance from hot coals, and temperature the day you are grilling.

Serve grilled bluefish hot on individual plates with tomato slices.

Nutritional Data

PER SERVING		EXCHANGES	
Calories	191	Milk	0.0
% Calories from fat	30	Veg.	0.5
Fat (gm)	6.2	Fruit	0.0
Sat. Fat (gm)	1.3	Bread	0.0
Cholesterol (mg)	83	Meat	3.5
Sodium (mg)	91	Fat	0.0
Protein (gm)	29.1		
Carbohydrate (gm)	3.6		

GROUPER *AU POIVRE* WITH BASIL SAUCE

Grouper can be interchanged with snapper. It is a firm fish, native to the Pacific Ocean.

Makes 4 servings

Basil Sauce

- 1 teaspoon olive oil
- 2 cloves garlic, minced
- ½ cup chopped onion
- 2 cups diced tomatoes
- 3 tablespoons fresh basil, *or* 1½ tablespoons dried
- ½ teaspoon thyme
- ¼ teaspoon each ingredient: salt and pepper

Grouper

- 4 5-oz. grouper fillets
- 2 teaspoons olive oil
- 1 tablespoon roughly cracked black pepper (to crack peppercorns, place them between two sheets of waxed paper and crush with rolling pin)
  Non-stick cooking spray

Basil Sauce: Heat oil in non-stick saucepan. Sauté garlic and onion, covered, over medium heat 3 minutes, stirring as necessary until onions are tender. Add tomatoes, basil, thyme, salt, and pepper. Simmer sauce, uncovered, 2 to 3 minutes, stirring occasionally. Sauce is good hot or cold.

Grouper: Brush fillets with oil. Sprinkle fish with cracked peppercorns, pressing them into flesh.

Arrange grouper on sprayed grill rack and place on grid over ashen-hot coals. Grill fish 3 minutes. Turn it and continue grilling about 2 minutes or until fish begins to flake when tested with a fork. Grilling time depends on thickness of fillets.

Serve hot grouper on individual dinner plates, spooning sauce around the fish. Good with a tossed salad.

Nutritional Data

PER SERVING		EXCHANGES	
Calories	198	Milk	0.0
% Calories from fat	24	Veg.	1.5
Fat (gm)	5.3	Fruit	0.0
Sat. Fat (gm)	0.9	Bread	0.0
Cholesterol (mg)	52	Meat	3.0
Sodium (mg)	204	Fat	0.0
Protein (gm)	28.9		
Carbohydrate (gm)	8.6		

Scrod with Fennel

Fennel has its season from October through March. Grilled fennel has a distinctive flavor. Shop for firm fennel bulbs. Remove stalks from bulb tops, and trim bottoms. Cut bulbs into ½-inch slices.

Scrod are light, delicate fish that are low in fat. They are actually young cod or haddock, which can be substituted. Scrod are fished off the North Atlantic coast of New England.

Makes 4 servings

Fennel
- 4 fennel bulbs, discard stalks, trim bottoms, slice
- 2 teaspoons canola oil
- 2 tablespoons chopped chives
- Non-stick cooking spray

Tarragon Brushing Sauce
- ½ cup apple cider
- 2 tablespoons fresh tarragon, *or* 1 tablespoon dried

Scrod
- ⅓ cup fennel seeds, soaked in water 30 minutes, drained (optional)
- 4 4-oz. scrod fillets
- 2 limes, sliced thin

Fennel take 20 to 25 minutes to grill, so put them on first. Brush the slices lightly with canola oil and sprinkle with chives.

Fennel: Arrange sprayed grill rack on grid over ashen-hot coals. Place fennel on grill rack and grill for 15 minutes. Turn slices over and continue grilling until fennel is soft. If slices become too dry, brush with tarragon brushing sauce. The fennel should be tender when done.

Tarragon Brushing Sauce: Combine cider and tarragon in small bowl.

Scrod: Sprinkle fennel seeds over hot coals for an aromatic effect. Brush scrod with tarragon brushing sauce. Place lime slices on sprayed grill rack positioned on grid over hot coals. Place fillets over fruit. Start fish after fennel has been grilling about 15 minutes. Grill scrod 3 to 5 minutes. Turn it with long-handled spatula, brush again with sauce, and continue grilling 2 to 3 minutes or until fish flakes easily when prodded with a fork.

Serve fennel with the fish fillets.

Nutritional Data

PER SERVING		EXCHANGES	
Calories	175	Milk	0.0
% Calories from fat	18	Veg.	0.0
Fat (gm)	3.5	Fruit	0.5
Sat. Fat (gm)	0.4	Bread	0.0
Cholesterol (mg)	62.4	Meat	3.0
Sodium (mg)	102	Fat	0.0
Protein (gm)	26.7		
Carbohydrate (gm)	10.1		

HALIBUT WITH PEACH CHUTNEY

Makes 4 servings

Peach Chutney

- 1 cup peeled, chopped peaches
- 1 tablespoon candied ginger, chopped
- ½ cup golden raisins
- ¼ lime, sliced thin
- ½ red onion, sliced thin
- ½ cup, packed, dark brown sugar
- ¼ cup red wine vinegar
- 1 clove garlic, minced
- ½ teaspoon dry mustard
- ¼ cup tomato sauce
- ¼ teaspoon each ingredient: ground cinnamon, ground allspice, and ground cloves

Halibut

- Butter-flavored non-stick cooking spray
- 4 halibut steaks, about 6 ozs. each

Peach Chutney: Combine all ingredients in heavy saucepan. Simmer 25 minutes, stirring occasionally until mixture is blended and thick. Cool. Spoon chutney into a bowl, cover, and refrigerate. Stir chutney before serving.

Halibut: Lightly spray halibut steaks. Spray grill rack and adjust it on grid over ashen-hot coals. Place halibut on rack. Grill fish about 4 minutes on each side or until done to taste. Remove steaks to individual plates, and spoon chutney over each serving. Serve hot.

Nutritional Data

PER SERVING		EXCHANGES	
Calories	397	Milk	0.0
% Calories from fat	9	Veg.	0.0
Fat (gm)	4.3	Fruit	2.0
Sat. Fat (gm)	0.6	Bread	1.5
Cholesterol (mg)	54.6	Meat	4.0
Sodium (mg)	201	Fat	0.0
Protein (gm)	36.9		
Carbohydrate (gm)	54.7		

GRILLED SEAFOOD PAELLA

Saffron is the stigma of a certain purple crocus. It is gathered by hand, making this the most expensive spice. Saffron imparts a beautiful yellow color to food. Crush the threads before using, or let a very small amount stand for a few minutes in a teaspoon of hot water, then discard the threads and keep the colored water to use in the recipe. Turmeric is used in many recipes as a substitute. Paella is a Spanish dish with saffron-flavored rice. It can have fish, chicken, sausage, or vegetables; this recipe uses grilled seafood and vegetables.

Makes 4 servings

Saffron Rice
- 1 teaspoon canola oil
- 1 cup long-grain rice
- 1¾ cups water
  Pinch of saffron, crushed, *or* ½ teaspoon turmeric
- ¼ teaspoon each ingredient: salt and pepper
- 1 cup fresh or defrosted peas

Seafood
- 8 mussels, scrubbed (do not use mussels or clams that are open before cooking)
- 8 clams, scrubbed
- 8 extra-large shrimp, shelled, deveined, washed, patted dry
- 8 ozs. red snapper fillets
- 1 red bell pepper, sliced
- 1 cup sliced tomatoes
- ½ cup sliced onion

Saffron Rice: Heat oil in a non-stick frying pan or in a paella pan. Sauté rice a few minutes over medium-low heat, stirring often. Mix in water, crushed saffron, salt, pepper, and peas. Bring mixture to a boil. Cover and reduce heat to simmer. Continue cooking about 20 minutes or until rice is cooked. Stir only once or twice, as necessary. Set aside. Reheat before serving.

Seafood: Spray grill rack and adjust it on grid over ashen-hot coals. Place mussels and clams on rack. If you can get seaweed from the fishmonger, arrange a small amount of it on the rack and set the shellfish on the seaweed. Cover grill and cook 5 minutes or until shellfish open. Discard any unopened mussels or clams. Place shellfish on warm rice.

Grill shrimp and fish on grill rack until cooked; turn shrimp once. The shrimp will be a pinkish white color, and the fish will flake easily when prodded with a fork. Place shrimp on the rice. Break fish into small pieces and scatter it over the rice.

At the same time you are grilling the shrimp and fish, grill the peppers, tomatoes, and onions. Grill tomatoes until hot, about 1 minute per side. Turn peppers once; they will char slightly when done, about 3 minutes. Grill onions until just charred, 2 to 4 minutes per side. Work quickly so that vegetables and seafood are done together. Add vegetables to the paella.

Stir the paella gently and serve with a crusty garlic bread.

Nutritional Data

PER SERVING		EXCHANGES	
Calories	360	Milk	0.0
% Calories from fat	9	Veg.	1.0
Fat (gm)	3.6	Fruit	0.0
Sat. Fat (gm)	0.5	Bread	3.0
Cholesterol (mg)	79.6	Meat	3.0
Sodium (mg)	323	Fat	0.0
Protein (gm)	29.9		
Carbohydrate (gm)	50		

Smoky Scallops and Wilted Spinach Salad

When grilling remember that times given are approximate because the actual cooking time depends on the thickness of the fish, the distance it is from the heat source, and the weather conditions on the day you are grilling. For example, fish will grill faster on a hot day than on a cold, windy day. So use the time stated as a guide, but watch the fish as it grills and do not overcook or you will loose flavor and tenderness.

Scallops are mollusks that are dredged from coastal waters. Select ones that are round, white, and large enough for grilling.

Makes 4 servings

Smoky Brushing Sauce
- ¼ cup cider vinegar
- 1 tablespoon canola oil
- ½ teaspoon liquid smoke
- 1 tablespoon grated lime peel
- 1 tablespoon dark brown sugar
- 1 bay leaf, crumbled

Scallops
- Non-stick cooking spray
- 1 lb. sea scallops

- 2 cups cooked brown rice
- **Wilted Spinach Salad** (recipe follows)

Smoky Brushing Sauce: Combine all ingredients in a small glass bowl. Brush scallops with sauce.

Scallops: Spray grill rack and position it on grid over ashen-hot coals. Grill scallops 2 minutes. Turn them with long-handled spatula and continue grilling until scallops become opaque; do not overcook. Brush scallops with sauce as they grill.

Remove scallops from grill and serve on individual plates with rice and wilted spinach salad.

Wilted Spinach Salad

- 2 teaspoons olive oil
- 2 cloves garlic, minced
- 1 tablespoon lemon juice
- 1 teaspoon grated lemon peel

2 teaspoons basil

¼ teaspoon each ingredient: salt and pepper

6 cups fresh spinach, washed well, drained,
dried, trimmed

1 cup sliced red onion
Non-stick cooking spray

3 slices day-old whole-wheat, *or* oatmeal bread,
cut into croutons

Using a small saucepan, mix together olive oil, garlic, lemon juice, lemon peel, basil, salt, and pepper. Heat dressing over medium heat only until hot.

Tear spinach into bite-sized pieces and place in salad bowl. Toss onions with spinach.

Heat a sprayed non-stick frying pan over medium heat. Cook croutons until toasted, turning with spatula, as necessary. Add croutons to salad bowl.

Drizzle hot dressing over salad, toss, and serve.

Nutritional Data

PER SERVING		EXCHANGES	
Calories	362	Milk	0.0
% Calories from fat	24	Veg.	2.0
Fat (gm)	10.1	Fruit	0.0
Sat. Fat (gm)	1	Bread	2.0
Cholesterol (mg)	48	Meat	3.0
Sodium (mg)	546	Fat	0.0
Protein (gm)	28.4		
Carbohydrate (gm)	42.3		

5.
POULTRY

Jerk Chicken Breasts with Grilled Pineapple

Grilled Chicken à la Budapest

Grilled Chicken Salad

Bow Tie Pasta and Grilled Chicken

Skinny Lickin' Smoked Chicken

Greek Chicken Grilled Over Grapevine

Grilled Chicken Lavender

3 Marinades for Grilled Chicken Breasts

Apple-Raisin-Stuffed Chicken Thighs

Chicken and Corn Burgers in Pitas

Blackened Chicken Breasts with Grilled Polenta

Turkey on a Stick

Mixed Grill with Tomato Relish and Mustard Sauce

JERK CHICKEN BREASTS WITH GRILLED PINEAPPLE

Jerk rub originated on the island of Jamaica. The rub is a spicy combination of flavors used to enhance the taste of meat and chicken during the marinating process. Here, it is used as interesting flavor combinations for the chicken.

Makes 4 servings

Jerk Rub
- ½ cup minced onion
- 2 teaspoons sugar
- 1 jalapeño pepper, carefully seeded, sliced
- ½ teaspoon coarse-ground black pepper
- ⅓ cup peeled, chopped pineapple
- 1 clove garlic, minced
- 1 tablespoon cider vinegar
- ¼ teaspoon each ingredient: red pepper flakes, thyme, ground allspice, and ground coriander

Chicken
- Non-stick cooking spray
- 4 small chicken breasts, about 4 ozs. each, skin and bones discarded
- 4 slices fresh pineapple
- 2 tablespoons fresh lime juice
- 4 teaspoons light brown sugar

Jerk Rub: Blend all rub ingredients in a food processor fitted with steel blade. Rub jerk seasonings over chicken. Place chicken in a shallow bowl and refrigerate 2 to 4 hours.

Chicken: Spray a grill rack and adjust it on grid over ashen-hot coals. Put chicken on rack. Cook about 10 minutes, turning once or twice as needed. Grill until chicken is cooked through but not overcooked.

While chicken is grilling, cook the pineapple. First sprinkle it with lime juice and a small amount of brown sugar. Grill pineapple about 2 minutes on each side. Pineapple should be hot.

Serve chicken hot with a slice of grilled pineapple.

Nutritional Data

PER SERVING		EXCHANGES	
Calories	144	Milk	0.0
% Calories from fat	13	Veg.	0.0
Fat (gm)	2.2	Fruit	1.0
Sat. Fat (gm)	0.6	Bread	0.0
Cholesterol (mg)	45.7	Meat	2.0
Sodium (mg)	43	Fat	0.0
Protein (gm)	17.3		
Carbohydrate (gm)	14.1		

GRILLED CHICKEN À LA BUDAPEST

Makes 6 servings

Bell Pepper Sauce (makes 1¼ cups)
- 1 teaspoon canola oil
- 3 cloves garlic, minced
- ¾ cup thinly sliced onion
- 3 red bell peppers, seeded and cut in thin strips
- 1 tablespoon Hungarian sweet paprika
- 1 cup fat-free chicken stock
- ¼ cup dry red wine
- 1 teaspoon fresh marjoram, *or* ½ teaspoon dried
- ¼ teaspoon each ingredient: salt and freshly ground black pepper
- 3 tablespoons tomato paste

Red Wine Marinade
- 1 cup dry red wine
- ¼ cup canola oil
- 2 cloves garlic, minced
- ¼ teaspoon freshly ground black pepper
- ½ teaspoon dried thyme

Chicken
- 1 whole fresh chicken, about 3 lbs., all visible fat discarded
- 1 apple, cored, sliced, in water pan for aromatic
- 3 cups hickory chips, soaked in water 30 minutes, drained

Bell Pepper Sauce: I prefer preparing the sauce in advance, but you can also prepare it while chicken is grilling. Heat oil in non-stick frying pan. Sauté garlic, onions, and bell pepper strips, covered, over medium heat 5 to 6 minutes or until tender; stir as needed. Sprinkle with paprika and stir in stock, wine, marjoram, salt, and pepper. Bring mixture to a boil. Stir in tomato paste. Reduce heat to simmer and continue cooking 3 minutes, stirring occasionally. Taste sauce to adjust seasonings. Reheat sauce before serving.

Red Wine Marinade: Combine all marinade ingredients and transfer to large plastic bag. Add chicken. Seal bag and turn it several times so that all parts of chicken are touched by marinade. Put bag in a large bowl and let stand at room temperature 1 hour, turning chicken once or twice.

Chicken: Prepare grill for indirect method. Arrange coals on either side of a drip pan, that is, any metal baking pan slightly larger than area occupied by food above it. Fill drip pan ¾ full of hot water and add apple slices. When coals are hot, sprinkle drained hickory chips over them.

Drain chicken of marinade and place it directly over drip pan. Cover grill. Grill chicken, breast side up, 1 hour, checking after 25 to 30 minutes to see if coals need replenishing.

To check for doneness, insert fork into deepest area of chicken thigh. The juices will run clear and joints will move easily when chicken is cooked. Remove skin, slice, and serve with warm red pepper sauce.

Nutritional Data

PER SERVING		EXCHANGES	
Calories	317	Milk	0.0
% Calories from fat	39	Veg.	1.0
Fat (gm)	13.9	Fruit	0.0
Sat. Fat (gm)	2.7	Bread	0.0
Cholesterol (mg)	102	Meat	4.5
Sodium (mg)	318	Fat	1.0
Protein (gm)	35.2		
Carbohydrate (gm)	10.9		

GRILLED CHICKEN SALAD

This recipe is a delicious combination of chilled salad with strips of hot grilled chicken. It is this unusual combination that makes it so interesting.

Makes 4 entree servings

Chicken

- 4 small chicken breasts, about 4 ozs. each, skin and bone discarded
- 1 cup fresh lime juice

Croutons

- Butter-flavored non-stick cooking spray
- 2 slices whole-wheat bread, trimmed
- 6 cloves garlic, minced

Salad

- 2 qts. crisp, cleaned mixed salad greens
- ½ cup plain non-fat yogurt
- ¼ cup low-calorie mayonnaise
- 2 teaspoons red wine vinegar
- 1½ teaspoons minced tarragon, *or* ¾ teaspoon dried
- ¼ teaspoon each ingredient: salt and freshly ground black pepper
- 4 teaspoons fresh-grated Parmesan cheese

Chicken: Place chicken breasts and lime juice in plastic bag and seal securely. Marinate 1 to 2 hours at room temperature, or leave in refrigerator as long as overnight. Turn chicken once or twice.

Croutons: While chicken is marinating, make croutons. Spray a non-stick frying pan. Cut bread into cubes. Sauté garlic and bread cubes a few minutes, turning as necessary until cubes are crisp and lightly browned. Cook over medium heat. Remove croutons and set aside.

Salad: Put greens in salad bowl. Mix yogurt, mayonnaise, vinegar, and tarragon in a small bowl. Toss dressing with greens. Sprinkle with salt and pepper. Chill salad until ready to serve.

Remove chicken from marinade. Place chicken breasts on sprayed grill rack over ashen-hot coals. Grill chicken about 10 minutes or until cooked to taste, turning once or twice with long-handled spatula. Remove chicken to cutting board and slice into strips.

Divide salad among 4 plates. Top with chicken strips, add croutons, and sprinkle with cheese.

Nutritional Data

PER SERVING		EXCHANGES	
Calories	415	Milk	0.0
% Calories from fat	26	Veg.	1.0
Fat (gm)	11.7	Fruit	0.0
Sat. Fat (gm)	3.3	Bread	0.5
Cholesterol (mg)	148	Meat	6.0
Sodium (mg)	546	Fat	0.0
Protein (gm)	59.7		
Carbohydrate (gm)	16		

Bow Tie Pasta and Grilled Chicken

This is a good recipe for leftover chicken or turkey.

Makes 4 entree servings

Rosemary Marinade

- ¼ cup olive oil
- ½ cup red wine vinegar, *or* tarragon vinegar
- 1 tablespoon capers
- ½ teaspoon garlic powder
- 1 tablespoon dried rosemary

Chicken, Pasta, and Vegetables

- 4 small chicken breasts, about 4 ozs. each, skin and bone discarded
- 3 cups bow tie pasta, cooked according to pkg. directions
- 1 cup grated carrots
- 2 large leeks, white and light green parts only, washed well
- ¼ teaspoon garlic powder
- 1 can (4 ozs.) diced green chilies
- ¼ cup chopped parsley
- 3 cups hickory chips, soaked in water 30 minutes, drained

Rosemary Marinade: Combine all marinade ingredients and pour into plastic bag. Add chicken breasts and seal bag securely. Turn bag several times so that all sides of chicken are touched by marinade. Place bag in a bowl and marinate 1 to 2 hours, turning bag once or twice.

While chicken is marinating, prepare bow ties and vegetables. Grate carrots and toss with cooked bow ties. Slice leeks and sauté in sprayed non-stick frying pan with garlic powder. Partially cover leeks and cook over medium heat 5 minutes or until tender. Stir leeks as necessary. Add leeks, chilies, and parsley to pasta and toss.

Drain chicken breasts and discard marinade. Sprinkle drained hickory chips over ashen-hot coals. Place chicken on sprayed grill rack and grill about 10 minutes or until done to taste. Remove chicken to cutting board and slice into strips. Toss chicken with pasta and serve.

Nutritional Data

PER SERVING		EXCHANGES	
Calories	339	Milk	0.0
% Calories from fat	20	Veg.	3.0
Fat (gm)	7.5	Fruit	0.0
Sat. Fat (gm)	1.3	Bread	2.0
Cholesterol (mg)	46	Meat	2.0
Sodium (mg)	411	Fat	0.0
Protein (gm)	23.4		
Carbohydrate (gm)	44.7		

SKINNY LICKIN' SMOKED CHICKEN

Don Hysko is that great and famous grill cook from Peoples Charcoal Woods, 75 Mill St., Cumberland, RI 02864, (800) 729-5800. "Peoples" sells pure hardwood charcoal, cooking woods, and smoking woods for perfect grilling results. This recipe is Don's personal one for chicken with a dry rub and a mop. Don's new technique of quick-smoking the food is introduced here. He adds soaked and drained chips at the end of the grilling process and covers the grill for a few minutes to produce a quick smoking process.

Makes 6 servings

6 small chicken breasts, about 4 ozs. each, skin and bone discarded, pounded lightly
Sugar maple charwood
3 cups Macintosh apple chips, soaked in water 30 minutes, drained

Dry Rub
1 tablespoon paprika
1 teaspoon sugar
½ teaspoon each ingredient: salt, freshly ground pepper, and onion powder
Pinch of fresh thyme
Pinch of cayenne pepper

Mopping Sauce
1 cup freshly squeezed orange juice
1 tablespoon Worcestershire sauce
3 tablespoons arrowroot, diluted slightly with water

Prepare grill, using sugar maple charwood.

Dry Rub: Combine ingredients in bowl. Rub chicken breasts and let them stand at room temperature about 15 minutes.

Mopping Sauce: Combine ingredients in small saucepan and simmer 5 minutes over low heat. Drizzle breasts with about one-third of mopping sauce.

Put chicken breasts on grill for about 20 minutes or until cooked thoroughly. Turn chicken once or twice, mopping at each turn.

In last five minutes of grilling, add apple chips to the fire and cover grill. (If grill does not have cover, invert a deep pan over grill to capture smoke flavor.)

Nutritional Data

PER SERVING		EXCHANGES	
Calories	116	Milk	0.0
% Calories from fat	17	Veg.	0.0
Fat (gm)	2.1	Fruit	0.0
Sat. Fat (gm)	0.6	Bread	0.0
Cholesterol (mg)	45.7	Meat	2.0
Sodium (mg)	243	Fat	0.0
Protein (gm)	17.3		
Carbohydrate (gm)	6.3		

GREEK CHICKEN GRILLED OVER GRAPEVINE

The ingredients in this recipe are typically Greek. Together, they create a light, easily grilled dinner. The recipe is easily doubled.

Makes 4 servings

Greek Island Sauce

- 1 cup plain non-fat yogurt
- 2 tablespoons grated lemon rind
- 2 tablespoons fresh oregano, *or* 1 tablespoon dried
- ½ teaspoon minced garlic
- ¼ cup chopped fresh parsley

Chicken

- Non-stick cooking spray
- 8 medium chicken drumsticks
- 1 lemon, sliced thin
- 1 qt. dried grapevine wood clippings, soaked in water 30 minutes, drained

Greek Island Sauce: In a small bowl, mix together yogurt, lemon rind, oregano, garlic, and parsley. Brush sauce over chicken legs. Place legs and sauce in plastic bag and seal securely. Marinate at room temperature 1 to 2 hours. Drain off marinade.

Chicken: Prepare grill, arranging the drained vine wood over hot coals. Spray the grid and replace it over ashen-hot coals.

Grill drumsticks, covered, 10 to 20 minutes, turning and grilling until cooked. To test for doneness, pierce legs; liquid should run clear and meat will feel tender. Discard skin before serving.

Remove grill cover last 5 minutes of cooking, and place lemon slices on sprayed grill rack. Cook lightly on each side, only until warm and beginning to color. Serve lemon wedges under chicken legs.

Nutritional Data

PER SERVING		EXCHANGES	
Calories	171	Milk	0.0
% Calories from fat	27	Veg.	0.0
Fat (gm)	5.1	Fruit	0.0
Sat. Fat (gm)	1.3	Bread	0.0
Cholesterol (mg)	82	Meat	3.0
Sodium (mg)	100	Fat	0.0
Protein (gm)	26.5		
Carbohydrate (gm)	4.9		

GRILLED CHICKEN LAVENDER

*This recipe was graciously contributed by Liz Clark of Iowa.
Liz is famous for her creative cooking classes and cooking tours.*

Makes 8 servings

- 8 chicken breasts, about 4 ozs. each, skin and bones discarded
- 1 tablespoon extra virgin olive oil
- 4 tablespoons lemon juice
- ½ cup minced parsley
- ½ cup minced lavender, flowers and leaves*

Place chicken breasts in a non-reactive dish large enough to contain them. Mix remaining ingredients for marinade and pour over chicken. Turn every half-hour for 3 hours.

Preheat grill until coals are ashen. Place chicken breasts on grill. Using tongs, turn chicken every 2 minutes for 8 minutes or until chicken is opaque and cooked through. Brush with marinade from time to time during grilling.

*Note: Nothing can instantly transport you to the south of France as quickly as the fragrance of lavender. Not only a sachet, it is also a culinary herb. Be sure to use fresh or dried lavender prepared for cooking purposes. Do not use the lavender from sachets as it has been chemically treated.

Nutritional Data

PER SERVING		EXCHANGES	
Calories	109	Milk	0.0
% Calories from fat	31	Veg.	0.0
Fat (gm)	3.6	Fruit	0.0
Sat. Fat (gm)	0.8	Bread	0.0
Cholesterol (mg)	46	Meat	2.0
Sodium (mg)	43.6	Fat	0.0
Protein (gm)	17		
Carbohydrate (gm)	1.1		

3 MARINADES FOR GRILLED CHICKEN BREASTS

The Cooking and Hospitality Institute of Chicago (CHIC) is one of the oldest and most respected professional cooking, restaurant, and hotel management schools in America. Thank you for these innovative marinade recipes to add zip to grilled or broiled chicken breasts.

The first is from North Africa and reflects the typical flavors of Moroccan cooking. The second marinade was developed by one of CHIC's students: it is a low fat version of classic teriyaki marinade. And the third is a light version of the classic marinade for chicken in northern India.

T o use each marinade, mix all ingredients in a large glass bowl. Add 2 to 4 chicken breasts and stir until they are well coated. Cover and refrigerate at least 2 hours, preferably overnight.

To grill, remove chicken from marinade, wiping any excess off chicken. Place breasts on a well-heated grill, and turn them several times during grilling so chicken cooks evenly for about 8 minutes without burning.

To broil, line a broiling rack with foil. Remove chicken from marinade, wiping any excess off chicken. Slide rack under a fully heated broiling unit and cook until done, about 8 minutes, turning several times so that chicken cooks evenly without burning.

Moroccan Marinade

½ cup finely chopped cilantro
2 garlic cloves, finely chopped
2 tablespoons hot Hungarian paprika
2 teaspoons ground cumin
  Juice of 1 lemon
½ cup chicken stock

Nutritional Data

PER SERVING		EXCHANGES	
Calories	7	Milk	0.0
% Calories from fat	27	Veg.	0.0
Fat (gm)	0.3	Fruit	0.0
Sat. Fat (gm)	0	Bread	0.0
Cholesterol (mg)	0	Meat	0.0
Sodium (mg)	15	Fat	0.0
Protein (gm)	0.5		
Carbohydrate (gm)	1.2		

Light Teriyaki Marinade

½ cup soy sauce
¼ cup chicken stock
¼ cup Madeira wine
2 tablespoons honey
  Zest of 1 orange, grated
2 large garlic cloves, finely chopped
2 tablespoons finely chopped ginger
  Freshly ground black pepper

Nutritional Data

PER SERVING		EXCHANGES	
Calories	25	Milk	0.0
% Calories from fat	2	Veg.	1.0
Fat (gm)	0	Fruit	0.0
Sat. Fat (gm)	0	Bread	0.0
Cholesterol (mg)	0	Meat	0.0
Sodium (mg)	695	Fat	0.0
Protein (gm)	0.8		
Carbohydrate (gm)	4.5		

Tandoori Marinade

4 ozs. onion, finely chopped
4 garlic cloves, finely chopped
  Ginger, 1-in. piece, finely chopped
  Juice of 1 lemon
1 cup plain non-fat yogurt
1 tablespoon ground coriander
1 teaspoon ground cumin
1 teaspoon ground turmeric

1 teaspoon garam masala (available in Indian
 markets)
¼ teaspoon ground cardamom
¼ teaspoon ground cloves
¼ teaspoon ground cinnamon
½ teaspoon salt
¼ teaspoon black pepper
¼ teaspoon cayenne

Nutritional Data

PER SERVING		EXCHANGES	
Calories	19	Milk	0.0
% Calories from fat	7	Veg.	1.0
Fat (gm)	0.1	Fruit	0.0
Sat. Fat (gm)	0	Bread	0.0
Cholesterol (mg)	0.3	Meat	0.0
Sodium (mg)	285	Fat	0.0
Protein (gm)	1.4		
Carbohydrate (gm)	3.4		

APPLE-RAISIN-STUFFED CHICKEN THIGHS

Apple stuffing adds a new taste to an old favorite—chicken. To heighten the flavor, use apple wood as an aromatic.

Makes 4 servings

Apple-Raisin Filling
- 2 tablespoons raisins
- 1 tablespoon dark rum
- Non-stick cooking spray
- ½ cup chopped onion
- 1 Granny Smith, *or* other firm baking apple, peeled, cored, chopped
- ½ teaspoon ground cinnamon
- 2 teaspoons sugar
- 1 cup whole-wheat breadcrumbs

Chicken
- 8 chicken thighs, boned, skin discarded
- ¼ cup apple juice, to brush chicken
- 3 handfuls dried apple twigs or wood, soaked in water 30 minutes, drained (optional)

Apple-Raisin Filling: Put raisins in small bowl and sprinkle with rum. Let raisins stand 20 minutes.

Heat a sprayed non-stick frying pan. Sauté onions and apples, covered, about 5 minutes over medium heat. Stir as necessary. Mix cinnamon and sugar together, and sprinkle over apple mixture. Toss in breadcrumbs and raisins.

Divide stuffing and fill pockets in chicken thighs.

Chicken: Scatter drained apple wood over ashen-hot coals and replace grid. Spray grill rack and position it on grid.

Brush chicken with apple juice. Grill thighs about 6 minutes on each side or until cooked. Grilling time depends on size and thickness of thighs. Turn chicken as necessary, brushing with apple juice each time.

Serve 2 chicken thighs on each plate.

Nutritional Data

PER SERVING		EXCHANGES	
Calories	388	Milk	0.0
% Calories from fat	30	Veg.	0.0
Fat (gm)	13	Fruit	1.0
Sat. Fat (gm)	3.5	Bread	1.5
Cholesterol (mg)	98	Meat	4.0
Sodium (mg)	326	Fat	0.0
Protein (gm)	30.8		
Carbohydrate (gm)	33.8		

CHICKEN AND CORN BURGERS IN PITAS

These burgers can also be served on lightly toasted hamburger buns, but we like them better in warm whole-wheat pita halves with all the trimmings.

Makes 4 servings

¾ lb. ground chicken breast

1 cup corn niblets, frozen and thawed

½ cup chopped green or red bell pepper

2 egg whites, slightly beaten

¼ cup chopped onion

¼ teaspoon each ingredient: salt and pepper
  Non-stick cooking spray

2 whole pita rounds, each cut in half to make 4 pockets

4 teaspoons low-calorie mayonnaise

4 lettuce leaves, washed, patted dry

4 tomato slices

4 thinly sliced onion rounds

½ cup alfalfa sprouts, *or* sprouts of your choice

4 semi-sour pickles, *or* pickle slices of your choice

T o make burgers, in a large mixing bowl, combine ground chicken, corn, peppers, egg whites, onions, salt, and pepper. Shape into 4 burgers (use a hamburger press if you have one). Place burgers on a plate and refrigerate until ready to grill.

Spray grill rack and set it on grid over ashen-hot coals. Grill chicken burgers 2 minutes on each side or until completely cooked. Burgers will char on the outside. Remove burgers from grill.

Warm pita halves on grill. Open pockets, brush with mayonnaise, and fill with lettuce, tomato, chicken burger, and onion. Sprinkle sprouts on top. Serve pickles on the side.

Nutritional Data

PER SERVING		EXCHANGES	
Calories	257	Milk	0.0
% Calories from fat	20	Veg.	0.0
Fat (gm)	5.8	Fruit	0.0
Sat. Fat (gm)	1.5	Bread	2.0
Cholesterol (mg)	39	Meat	2.0
Sodium (mg)	609	Fat	0.0
Protein (gm)	20.9		
Carbohydrate (gm)	31		

BLACKENED CHICKEN BREASTS WITH GRILLED POLENTA

The concept of blackening food comes to us from the Cajun area of Louisiana. It is usually used on fish, but here we blacken chicken for a spicy, tasty treat. Polenta is a firm, seasoned cornmeal pudding that is cut into strips and served as a side dish. The only caution with polenta is to make sure it does not have any lumps. Add cornmeal in a thin stream, and whisk constantly for a lump-free mixture.

Makes 4 servings

Blackening Rub

- 1 tablespoon sweet paprika
- 2 teaspoons onion flakes
- ½ teaspoon each ingredient: garlic powder and oregano
- ¼ teaspoon each ingredient: salt and cayenne

Chicken

- 4 small chicken breasts, about 4 ozs. each, boned, skin discarded
  Butter-flavored non-stick cooking spray
- 1 cup plain non-fat yogurt
  Grilled Herbed Polenta (recipe follows)

Blackening Rub: In small glass bowl, mix paprika, onion flakes, garlic powder, oregano, salt, and cayenne.

Chicken: Wash chicken pieces and pat dry. Spray chicken lightly on both sides. Sprinkle chicken with blackening rub, patting the rub to make sure it adheres to the chicken. Put chicken on a plate, cover lightly, and refrigerate until ready to grill.

Spray grill rack and adjust it on grid, over ashen-hot coals. Place chicken on rack and grill 8 to 10 minutes, turning once or twice as needed. Grill until chicken is cooked through but not overcooked.

Remove chicken breasts with long-handled spatula to individual plates. Serve hot with yogurt and polenta.

Grilled Herbed Polenta

- 4½ cups water
- 1 cup cornmeal
- ½ teaspoon each ingredient: basil and thyme
- ¼ teaspoon white pepper
  Non-stick cooking spray

Bring lightly salted water to a boil in saucepan. Reduce water to simmer. Pour cornmeal into water in a slow steady stream, whisking constantly.

Stir in basil, thyme, and pepper. Continue whisking or mixing with a heavy spoon. Cook about 20 minutes or until smooth and thickened.

Spray a 9 × 13-inch pan. Pour cooked polenta into pan, spreading evenly. Cool. Cut cooled polenta into serving-size pieces.

Grill polenta on a sprayed grill rack over ashen-hot coals. Grill only until warmed, 1 to 2 minutes on each side. Polenta will be hot and crusty.

Nutritional Data

PER SERVING		EXCHANGES	
Calories	242	Milk	0.0
% Calories from fat	13	Veg.	0.0
Fat (gm)	3.4	Fruit	0.0
Sat. Fat (gm)	0.8	Bread	2.0
Cholesterol (mg)	47	Meat	2.0
Sodium (mg)	228	Fat	0.0
Protein (gm)	22.9		
Carbohydrate (gm)	30.1		

TURKEY ON A STICK

This is a good recipe to serve children. You can also shape the turkey into burgers and grill to taste.

Makes 4 servings

- 1 lb. ground skinless turkey breast
- 1 tablespoon dried onion
- 2 teaspoons low-sodium soy sauce
- ¼ cup chopped green bell pepper
- ½ teaspoon Worcestershire sauce
- ¼ teaspoon pepper
- 8 wooden skewers, soaked in water 30 minutes, drained
- Non-stick cooking spray

I n large bowl, combine turkey, onions, soy sauce, pepper, Worcestershire sauce, and pepper. Wipe skewers. Using your clean hands, mold about ¼ cup of turkey mixture around each skewer.

Spray a grill rack and place it on grid over ashen-hot coals. Place turkey skewers on grill rack. Cook about 7 minutes, turning skewers carefully every 2 minutes. Use a spatula to gently loosen them if they begin to stick to grill. Using a long-handled spatula, transfer skewers to serving plate. Serve hot with mustard.

Nutritional Data

PER SERVING		EXCHANGES	
Calories	122	Milk	0.0
% Calories from fat	18	Veg.	0.5
Fat (gm)	2.3	Fruit	0.0
Sat. Fat (gm)	0.7	Bread	0.0
Cholesterol (mg)	50	Meat	2.0
Sodium (mg)	140	Fat	0.0
Protein (gm)	21.9		
Carbohydrate (gm)	2.3		

MIXED GRILL WITH TOMATO RELISH AND MUSTARD SAUCE

The mixed grill usually consists of red meat: one chop, one sausage, and maybe one slice of steak for each person. This English dish has been adapted for poultry.

Makes 4 servings

Tomato Relish

- 1 lb., about 3 large, tomatoes, peeled, seeded, chopped
- 1 teaspoon olive oil
- 2 cloves garlic, minced
- ½ teaspoon dried marjoram
- 3 tablespoons balsamic vinegar

Mustard Sauce

- ⅓ cup prepared English mustard
- 1 tablespoon light brown sugar
- 1 tablespoon dark beer

Meats

- 2 turkey, *or* chicken, spicy sausages
- ½ lb. ground turkey breast
- 1½ cups whole-wheat breadcrumbs
- ½ cup chopped onion
- ¼ teaspoon garlic powder
- Non-stick cooking spray

Tomato Relish: In large mixing bowl, toss together tomatoes, oil, garlic, marjoram, and vinegar. Cover and refrigerate until serving time.

Mustard Sauce: Stir together mustard, sugar, and beer. Taste to adjust sugar. Cover and set aside until ready to serve.

Meats: Prick sausages with tip of knife a few times. Place near grill. Mix together remaining ingredients, except cooking spray, and shape into 4 burgers. Cover and refrigerate until grilling time.

Spray grill rack and place on grid over ashen-hot coals. Grill sausages and burgers on both sides, turning carefully with long-handled spatula. Rotate sausages every 3 minutes for 9 to 12 minutes or until done. Grill burgers 2 minutes on each side, and then continue grilling about 6 minutes or until done. Turn as necessary.

To serve, cut sausages in slices and put them on individual plates along with a burger. Spoon tomato relish and a dollop of mustard sauce on each plate. Serve hot.

Nutritional Data

PER SERVING		EXCHANGES	
Calories	337	Milk	0.0
% Calories from fat	23	Veg.	2.5
Fat (gm)	8.7	Fruit	0.0
Sat. Fat (gm)	1.7	Bread	2.0
Cholesterol (mg)	36.2	Meat	2.0
Sodium (mg)	751	Fat	0.5
Protein (gm)	20.6		
Carbohydrate (gm)	44.5		

6.
MEATS

Pork Loin with 5-Minute Barbecue Sauce
Pork Chops, Apple Slices, and Potatoes
Butterflied Pork Chops with Mushrooms
Lamb Shish Kabob
Grilled Loin of Lamb
Beef Kabobs Over Rice and Noodle Pilaf
Steak Kabobs with Ranchero Sauce
Meat Loaf on the Grill
Grilled Steak Salad
Grilled Buffalo Burgers
Mushroom Garden Burgers

PORK LOIN WITH 5-MINUTE BARBECUE SAUCE

The barbecue sauce can easily be doubled and given as a gift to a good friend.

Makes 6 servings

Orange-Lime Marinade
- ¾ cup fresh orange juice
- ¼ cup fresh lime juice
- ¼ cup chopped onion
- 3 cloves garlic, minced
- Dash Worcestershire sauce

Pork
- 1½ lbs. pork loin, trim any visible fat
- Non-stick cooking spray

5-Minute Barbecue Sauce
- 1 tablespoon grated orange peel
- 1 medium red onion, peeled, cut into quarters
- 3 cloves garlic, peeled
- 1½ cups tomato juice
- ¼ cup fresh orange juice
- ¼ cup ketchup
- 2 tablespoons honey
- 2 teaspoons Worcestershire sauce
- 1 tablespoon chili powder
- ¼ teaspoon liquid smoke (optional)
- ½ teaspoon paprika
- ¼ teaspoon red pepper flakes
- ¼ teaspoon salt

Black Beans
- 3 cups cooked black beans

Orange-Lime Marinade: Combine all ingredients in small bowl. Place pork loin in plastic bag. Add marinade and seal bag securely. Turn bag several times so that all surfaces of pork are covered with marinade. Put bag in flat dish and marinate 2 to 3 hours. Turn bag once or twice while marinating.

5-Minute Barbecue Sauce: Prepare while pork loin is marinating. Use food processor fitted with steel blade, or use blender. Chop together orange peel, onion, and cloves. Add remaining ingredients and process until sauce is smooth.

Pork: Spray grill rack and place it on grid over ashen-hot coals. Remove pork loin from marinade, drain, and put on grill rack. Discard marinade. Grill pork about 6 minutes on each of its 3 or 4 sides or until done in center. Brush pork with barbecue sauce as it is cooking.

Remove loin to carving board, and let it rest 5 minutes. Slice thin and drizzle barbecue sauce over pork. Serve with hot black beans.

Nutritional Data

PER SERVING		EXCHANGES	
Calories	323	Milk	0.0
% Calories from fat	23	Veg.	2.0
Fat (gm)	8.3	Fruit	0.5
Sat. Fat (gm)	2.7	Bread	1.5
Cholesterol (mg)	51	Meat	2.5
Sodium (mg)	515	Fat	0.0
Protein (gm)	25.1		
Carbohydrate (gm)	38.7		

Pork Chops, Apple Slices, and Potatoes

Apple goes well with pork. Use thin, well trimmed pork chops. This recipe works well on the indoor grill (use according to the manufacturer's directions), which can be a wonderful addition to your cooking aids. It's the only way to obtain a true grill flavor and yet cook right on your kitchen range.

Makes 4 servings

Non-stick cooking spray

4 baking potatoes, washed, cut into quarters, partially cooked

4 thin lean pork chops, all visible fat removed

1 teaspoon thyme

½ cup dried thyme, soaked in water 5 minutes, drained, for aromatic (optional)

2 Granny Smith apples, cored, sliced

2 tablespoons fresh lemon juice

1 tablespoon sugar

P osition sprayed grid over ashen-hot coals. Spray potatoes lightly and grill 15 minutes or until done to taste, turning with long-handled spatula every 5 minutes. Potatoes should be tender and browned.

After 10 minutes of grilling potatoes, lightly spray pork chops and place them on grid. Sprinkle with thyme. Sprinkle thyme over hot coals. Grill chops about 3 minutes on each side or until done to taste. All signs of pink should be gone from center of chops.

After you put the chops on the grill, sprinkle apple slices with lemon juice and sugar. Put apple slices on sprayed grill rack and place on grid. Grill apple slices about 1 minute on each side.

Serve hot potato wedges, pork chops, and apples on individual plates.

Nutritional Data

PER SERVING		EXCHANGES	
Calories	445	Milk	0.0
% Calories from fat	21	Veg.	0.0
Fat (gm)	10.6	Fruit	1.0
Sat. Fat (gm)	3.6	Bread	3.0
Cholesterol (mg)	63	Meat	2.5
Sodium (mg)	66	Fat	0.5
Protein (gm)	23.3		
Carbohydrate (gm)	65.6		

BUTTERFLIED PORK CHOPS WITH MUSHROOMS

Pork gets tough if overcooked on the grill, and yet it should not be undercooked, so watch the meat as it grills. If chanterelle mushrooms are not available, use a variety of your choice.

Makes 4 servings

⅓ cup dried chanterelle, *or* other dried mushrooms, picked over, trimmed

4 boneless pork loin chops, about 1 lb., butterflied

Light Chanterelle Sauce

1 teaspoon butter

1 cup fresh chanterelles, picked over, sliced

1 clove garlic, minced

4 large shallots, minced

½ cup dry sherry, *or* Madeira

¼ teaspoon each ingredient: salt and pepper

3 cups cooked rice

Put dried mushrooms on cookie sheet and bake 20 minutes or until mushrooms are firm, at preheated 275°. Process mushrooms until they are "dust." Let settle a few minutes before transferring from food processor to a bowl. Sprinkle and press mushroom dust onto pork chops. Place chops on a plate and let stand 30 minutes.

Light Chanterelle Sauce: While pork chops are standing, prepare sauce. Melt butter in non-stick frying pan. Sauté fresh chanterelles, garlic, and shallots about 5 minutes over medium heat, partially covered, until mushrooms are cooked. Stir mushrooms as needed. Stir in wine, salt, and pepper. Serve hot.

Position grill rack on grid over ashen-hot coals. Grill chops about 3 minutes on each side or until done to taste. All signs of pink should be gone from centers of chops.

Serve each chop drizzled with mushroom sauce, and a helping of rice.

Nutritional Data

PER SERVING		EXCHANGES	
Calories	424	Milk	0.0
% Calories from fat	28	Veg.	2.5
Fat (gm)	13.1	Fruit	0.0
Sat. Fat (gm)	4.7	Bread	2.0
Cholesterol (mg)	75.1	Meat	3.0
Sodium (mg)	204	Fat	1.0
Protein (gm)	25.8		
Carbohydrate (gm)	41.2		

Lamb Shish Kabob

One of the first grilled meats surely must have been shish kabob over an open fire. Imagine the herdsmen gathered around a fire to keep warm. Which one thought of sticking a piece of meat at the end of a stick and cooking it over the fire? Whoever it was, we are grateful.

Makes 4 servings

Lime Marinade

- ½ cup fresh lime juice
- 2 tablespoons olive oil
- ¼ cup minced green onion
- ½ teaspoon garlic powder
- ¼ teaspoon cayenne pepper

Kabobs

- 1 lb. lamb roast, cut into 1½-in. cubes
- 1 lb. small, red new potatoes, washed, almost cooked, drained
- 4 green onions, trimmed, cut into 2-in. pieces
- 12 cherry tomatoes
- 1 onion, peeled, cut into wedges
- 3 cups mesquite chips, *or* other aromatic wood of your choice, soaked in water 30 minutes, drained
  Non-stick cooking spray

Lime Marinade: Combine all marinade ingredients in small glass bowl. Put lamb pieces and marinade in plastic bag. Seal bag securely. Turn bag several times so that all parts of meat are touched with marinade. Place bag in deep bowl and put it in refrigerator. Marinate 4 hours or as long as overnight.

Kabobs: Thread drained lamb, potatoes, green onions, tomatoes, and onion wedges evenly onto 4 skewers.

Scatter drained mesquite chips over ashen-hot coals. Replace sprayed grid onto grill. Grill kabobs 10 to 12 minutes, turning every 3 to 4 minutes. Remove one kabob and cut into meat to check doneness. Continue grilling kabobs until done to taste.

Nutritional Data

PER SERVING		EXCHANGES	
Calories	287	Milk	0.0
% Calories from fat	23	Veg.	1.0
Fat (gm)	7.5	Fruit	0.0
Sat. Fat (gm)	2.1	Bread	1.5
Cholesterol (mg)	57	Meat	2.5
Sodium (mg)	54	Fat	0.0
Protein (gm)	21.6		
Carbohydrate (gm)	33.9		

GRILLED LOIN OF LAMB

Elizabeth Clark, "the First Lady of Iowa cuisine," has sent us her easy recipe for grilled loin of lamb with rosemary. Couscous, risotto, or polenta are all noteworthy Mediterranean side dishes to accompany this entree.

Makes 4 servings

1   small loin of lamb, about 1 lb., trimmed of
    visible fat
    Sea salt (optional)
    Pepper, freshly ground (optional)
3   cups couscous, cooked according to pkg.
    directions
    Rosemary sprigs, for garnish

Preheat grill until white char shows on outside of coals. Gently sprinkle salt and freshly ground pepper over lamb. Place lamb on grid and cook, turning after 5 minutes. Grill until internal temperature registers 130° on an instant-read thermometer. Remove meat to carving board, cover with foil, and allow to rest 10 minutes.

With sharp knife, slice lamb on the diagonal into ¼-inch-thick slices. Place slices on each of 4 prewarmed dinner plates. Garnish with sprigs of fresh rosemary.

Serve lamb with hot couscous.

Nutritional Data

PER SERVING		EXCHANGES	
Calories	273	Milk	0.0
% Calories from fat	18	Veg.	0.0
Fat (gm)	5.2	Fruit	0.0
Sat. Fat (gm)	1.8	Bread	2.0
Cholesterol (mg)	57	Meat	2.5
Sodium (mg)	51	Fat	0.0
Protein (gm)	23.3		
Carbohydrate (gm)	31.2		

BEEF KABOBS OVER RICE AND NOODLE PILAF

This entire meal is easy to prepare if you thread the kabobs ahead of time and refrigerate them until ready to grill.

Makes 4 servings

Rice and Noodle Pilaf

Butter-flavored non-stick cooking spray

½ cup thin noodles, *or* spaghetti, uncooked, broken into small pieces

1 cup long-grain rice, uncooked

1 cup chicken stock

Kabobs

Olive-oil-flavored non-stick cooking spray

¾ lb. well-trimmed beef sirloin, cut into 1-in. chunks

1 teaspoon crumbled rosemary

4 long skewers, *or* double-pronged skewers

16 cherry tomatoes, whole

1 large onion, cut in half, pieces separated

8 large white or brown mushroom caps, cleaned

2 large red or green bell peppers, seeded, cut into squares suitable for skewers

Rice and Noodle Pilaf: Heat sprayed non-stick frying pan. Sauté uncooked noodles over medium heat until browned, stirring often and not overcooking. Add uncooked rice and stir to combine it with noodles. Stir in stock and simmer, stirring occasionally, until stock is absorbed and rice is tender, about 20 minutes. Cover and let stand until ready to serve. Reheat before serving.

Kabobs: Spray kabobs lightly and dust with rosemary. Thread, with vegetables, onto skewers, adding extra vegetables at ends of skewers.

Spray grill rack and place it on grid over ashen-hot coals. Grill kabobs 10 to 12 minutes, turning every 3 to 4 minutes. Remove one kabob and cut into meat to check doneness. Continue grilling kabobs until done to taste. Serve hot with the pilaf.

Nutritional Data

PER SERVING		EXCHANGES	
Calories	442	Milk	0.0
% Calories from fat	21	Veg.	3.0
Fat (gm)	10	Fruit	0.0
Sat. Fat (gm)	3.6	Bread	3.0
Cholesterol (mg)	75.6	Meat	3.0
Sodium (mg)	74	Fat	0.0
Protein (gm)	30.1		
Carbohydrate (gm)	53.4		

Steak Kabobs with Ranchero Sauce

Unless otherwise indicated, use long skewers, 10 to 12 inches in length. Double-pronged skewers are a great help. They keep the food from slipping around. If double skewers are not available, you can substitute two single skewers for a similar effect. Also, at the end of summer when the stems on your garden herbs are thick and woody, you can use them for skewers. Cut them off at the correct length, remove leaves and branches, and cut one end into a point. Mint, basil, thyme, oregano, and rosemary make my favorite skewers. You might want to wrap the pointed ends in foil so they do not burn during grilling.

Makes 4 servings

Easy Marinade

- ⅓ cup fresh lemon juice
- 2 tablespoons canola oil
- 3 tablespoons balsamic vinegar
- ½ teaspoon powdered ginger

- 1 lb. flank steak, cut into 1-in.-wide pieces, about 2½ in. long

Ranchero Sauce

- Non-stick cooking spray
- 4 cloves garlic, minced
- ½ cup chopped onion
- 1 cup chopped red tomatoes
- 2 red or green bell peppers, seeded, chopped
- 1 jalapeño pepper, carefully seeded, chopped
- ½ teaspoon cumin
- ¼ cup tomato juice

Kabobs

- 4 ears corn, silk removed, cut into 2-in. rounds
- 8 large mushroom caps

- ½ cup bay leaves, soaked in water 5 minutes, drained for aromatic (optional)

Easy Marinade: Combine all marinade ingredients in small glass bowl. Put meat pieces and marinade into plastic bag. Seal bag securely. Turn bag several times so that all parts of meat are touched with marinade. Place bag in deep bowl and put in refrigerator. Marinate meat 4 hours or as long as overnight.

Ranchero Sauce: While meat is marinating prepare the sauce. Heat a sprayed non-stick saucepan over medium heat. Sauté garlic and onions for a few minutes, covered. Stir as necessary. Add tomatoes, peppers, and cumin. Sauté, uncovered, 5 minutes. If pan is too dry, cover vegetables with water and continue cooking until vegetables are soft. Stir in tomato juice. Set sauce aside.

Kabobs: Thread 4 skewers, beginning with a piece of corn and including steak and 2 mushroom caps per skewer, until all food has been threaded.

Scatter drained bay leaves over ashen-hot coals. Replace sprayed grid onto grill. Grill kabobs 10 to 12 minutes, turning every 3 to 4 minutes. Remove one kabob and cut into meat to check doneness. Continue grilling kabobs until done to taste.

Put a skewer on each plate, and drizzle ranchero sauce over kabobs. Serve hot.

Nutritional Data

PER SERVING		EXCHANGES	
Calories	368	Milk	0.0
% Calories from fat	26	Veg.	1.0
Fat (gm)	11.1	Fruit	0.0
Sat. Fat (gm)	3.6	Bread	2.0
Cholesterol (mg)	45.7	Meat	4.0
Sodium (mg)	114	Fat	0.0
Protein (gm)	33.1		
Carbohydrate (gm)	38.7		

MEAT LOAF ON THE GRILL

Why not grill meat loaf slices. It can be leftover meat loaf or meat loaf prepared with grilling as the objective.

Makes 4 servings

Non-stick cooking spray
1 cup sliced mushrooms
½ lb. ground veal, *or* beef
⅓ lb. ground leanest pork
⅓ cup fresh whole-wheat breadcrumbs
¼ cup egg substitute
¼ cup chopped onion
½ cup peeled, chopped tomato
½ teaspoon each ingredient: tarragon, thyme, allspice
¼ teaspoon each ingredient: salt, pepper, cinnamon
½ cup heaping alfalfa sprouts, *or* mixed sprouts of your choice

H eat a sprayed non-stick frying pan over medium heat. Sauté mushrooms, covered, about 4 minutes. Stir as necessary. Drain. Transfer mushrooms to a large mixing bowl.

Add remaining ingredients and mix well.

Spray a 3½ × 7 × 2-inch loaf pan. Mound filling into pan. Preheat oven to 325°. Bake meat loaf 1 hour in center of oven or until juices run clear. Cool. Slice meat loaf when you are ready to grill.

Spray grill rack and place it on grid over ashen-hot coals. Grill meat loaf slices on both sides, turning carefully with a long-handled spatula. You want only to warm the meat loaf and have it obtain a grilled, smoky flavor. Remove hot meat loaf slices from grill and serve.

Nutritional Data

PER SERVING		EXCHANGES	
Calories	135	Milk	0.0
% Calories from fat	25	Veg.	0.5
Fat (gm)	3.7	Fruit	0.0
Sat. Fat (gm)	1.3	Bread	0.0
Cholesterol (mg)	62	Meat	2.5
Sodium (mg)	226	Fat	0.0
Protein (gm)	19.4		
Carbohydrate (gm)	5.8		

GRILLED STEAK SALAD

Hot, spicy, thin slices of grilled beef when served as part of a salad make a complete meal.

Makes 4 entree servings

Salad
- 4 cups assorted greens, washed, dried
- 2 large tomatoes, sliced
- ½ cup thinly sliced red onion
- 1 cup snow peas, trimmed
- ¾ cup fat-free Italian dressing
- Non-stick cooking spray
- 1 cup day-old whole-wheat bread cubes
- ½ teaspoon powdered garlic

Hot Mopping Sauce
- ¾ cup red wine vinegar
- ¼ cup fresh lime, *or* lemon juice
- 2 jalapeño peppers, carefully seeded, chopped
- 1 teaspoon Worcestershire sauce
- 1 green onion, minced
- ¼ teaspoon cayenne pepper
- ¾ cup crushed tomatoes, include juice

Steak
- ¾ lb. leanest flank steak

Salad: Arrange greens, tomatoes, onions, and snow peas on dinner plates. Cover and refrigerate until needed. Sprinkle with dressing before serving.

Heat a sprayed non-stick frying pan over medium heat. Add bread cubes sprinkled with garlic. Cook over medium heat, stirring occasionally until bread cubes are slightly toasted. Remove cubes and set aside until serving time.

Hot Mopping Sauce: Heat a sprayed non-stick frying pan over medium heat. Add all mopping ingredients. Bring ingredients to a boil, stirring occasionally.

Steak: Mop the steak and place it in a glass container for 1 hour. Set steak on grid over hot coals. Add soaked and drained hickory chips to hot coals if desired. Cook steak 5 to 7 minutes on each side or until done to taste. Steak should be slightly pink in center. Continue to mop steak as you are grilling.

Remove steak to cutting board, and allow meat to stand 5 minutes. Cut meat across the grain into thin slices. Arrange meat slices over salad, and sprinkle on croutons. Serve while meat is hot.

Nutritional Data

PER SERVING		EXCHANGES	
Calories	244	Milk	0.0
% Calories from fat	24	Veg.	2.0
Fat (gm)	6.5	Fruit	0.0
Sat. Fat (gm)	2.5	Bread	0.5
Cholesterol (mg)	34	Meat	3.0
Sodium (mg)	742	Fat	0.0
Protein (gm)	24.5		
Carbohydrate (gm)	22		

GRILLED BUFFALO BURGERS

Buffalo is lower in fat than most red meats but still tender and flavorful, as it now is raised for food. Buffalo is becoming available in the frozen food sections of large supermarkets. But if you can't find it, substitute the leanest ground meat. Buy the meat separately and have the butcher grind it for you.

Makes 4 servings

- 1 lb. ground buffalo meat, *or* lean ground beef
- ¼ cup chopped green onion
- ½ teaspoon garlic powder
- ¼ teaspoon each ingredient: salt and pepper
- 1 cup whole-wheat breadcrumbs
- ½ cup grated carrot
- 1 egg white
  Non-stick cooking spray
- 4 French rolls, open
  Stone-ground mustard, to taste (optional)
- ½ cup minced onion, for garnish
- 2 jalapeño peppers, carefully seeded, chopped, for garnish (optional)

P ut the buffalo meat in a deep mixing bowl. Mix in green onions, garlic powder, salt, pepper, breadcrumbs, carrot, and egg white. Blend all ingredients. Shape into 4 burgers and refrigerate until ready to use.

Spray grill rack and place it on grid over ashen-hot coals. Grill burgers 3 minutes on each side, or until done to taste, turning carefully with a long-handled spatula. Burgers will crust slightly. Remove burgers from grill.

Toast rolls. Spread bottom of roll with mustard to taste. Add burger, chopped onion, and jalapeño peppers. Serve hot.

Nutritional Data

PER SERVING		EXCHANGES	
Calories	355	Milk	0.0
% Calories from fat	14	Veg.	0.0
Fat (gm)	5.3	Fruit	0.0
Sat. Fat (gm)	1.5	Bread	2.0
Cholesterol (mg)	75	Meat	4.0
Sodium (mg)	668	Fat	0.0
Protein (gm)	33.7		
Carbohydrate (gm)	40.8		

MUSHROOM GARDEN BURGERS

The all-time grill favorite is the hamburger. So here is our version, a lighter mushroom garden burger.

Makes 4 servings

½ lb. leanest ground beef (select the meat and ask the butcher to grind it for you)

1 lb. cultivated mushrooms, trimmed, chopped, and squeezed dry in paper towels

½ cup chopped green or red bell peppers

½ cup chopped onion

1½ cups cooked brown rice

1 egg white, slightly beaten

1 teaspoon marjoram

½ teaspoon garlic powder
  Non-stick cooking spray

4 hamburger rolls

4 teaspoons low-calorie mayonnaise

4 leaves romaine lettuce, washed, drained

4 slices tomato

I n large bowl, combine hamburger, mushrooms, peppers, onions, brown rice, egg white, marjoram, and garlic powder. Shape into 4 patties. Put patties on a plate, cover, and refrigerate until grilling time.

Spray grill rack and set it on grid over ashen-hot coals. Grill burgers 2 minutes on each side, then about 6 minutes until done, turning carefully with a long-handled spatula. Burgers will crust slightly. Remove burgers from grill.

Toast rolls on grill. Spread bottom of rolls with mayonnaise. Tear lettuce to size and arrange on rolls. Add burgers, top with tomato slices, and serve.

Nutritional Data

PER SERVING		EXCHANGES	
Calories	348	Milk	0.0
% Calories from fat	21	Veg.	2.0
Fat (gm)	8.4	Fruit	0.0
Sat. Fat (gm)	2.5	Bread	2.5
Cholesterol (mg)	32	Meat	2.0
Sodium (mg)	326	Fat	0.0
Protein (gm)	20.3		
Carbohydrate (gm)	48.8		

7.

SMOKED FOODS

Smoked Turkey with Mushroom Rub

Smoked Turkey with Sun-Dried Tomato Dust

Turkey Breast with Georgia Peach Mop

Smoked Turkey Sausages with Caramelized Onions

Lime-Ginger Smoked Salmon

Smoked Whitefish with Herb Dressing

Hickory-Smoked Shrimp Dip with Crudités

Smoked Mussels with Caponata Relish

Barbecue Pork Sandwich with Whiskey-Baked Beans

Smoked Southwest Back Ribs with Refried Beans

Pecos River Beef Brisket with Barbecue Sauce and Rice

For information about smoker grills, see page 3.

123

Smoked Turkey with Mushroom Rub

Makes 12 servings

1 pkg. (4 ozs.) mixed dried mushrooms
4–5 handfuls dry apple, plum, or hickory twigs or
  chips
2 apples, sliced, for aromatic
1 turkey breast, about 6 lbs., bone in, skin
  discarded, wash turkey and pat dry

T o make "dust" you must further dry out, to a crisp stage, already dried vegetables. In this case we are drying out mushrooms. Preheat oven to 250°. Arrange mushrooms on baking sheet. Bake mushrooms in center of oven 30 minutes or until they are crisp but not burned. Puree mushrooms in food processor until they are "dust." Let dust settle a few minutes, then remove and store in shallow bowl, covered.

Soak twigs or chips in water 25 to 30 minutes; drain. While twigs are soaking, prepare smoker according to manufacturer's directions. Fill fire pan about three-quarters full of hardwood charcoal and heat coals until hot. Arrange twigs over hot coals. Fill water pan of smoker half-way with hot water, add apple slices, and place it in smoker.

Wash turkey and pat dry. Rub turkey with dried mushroom dust.

Cover smoker and let turkey smoke 5 to 6 hours until internal temperature reaches 160°. Add more charcoal and hot water as necessary during smoking period. Be sure turkey is cooked through. To check for doneness, stick tip of small, sharp knife into turkey; juices should run clear. Or use a meat thermometer. Allow turkey to stand at room temperature 10 minutes before slicing. Smoked turkey is good warm or cold.

While smoking, remember not to remove lid of smoker more than is necessary because it allows heat and moisture to escape and slows the smoking process. Also, remember to use pot holders when removing parts of the smoker to add more charcoal or hot water.

Nutritional Data

PER SERVING		EXCHANGES	
Calories	189	Milk	0.0
% Calories from fat	17	Veg.	0.0
Fat (gm)	3.5	Fruit	0.0
Sat. Fat (gm)	1.1	Bread	0.0
Cholesterol (mg)	71	Meat	3.5
Sodium (mg)	67	Fat	0.0
Protein (gm)	32.1		
Carbohydrate (gm)	5.5		

SMOKED TURKEY WITH SUN-DRIED TOMATO DUST

Turkey is one of the foods that smokes very well. So think of an excuse for a party and smoke a turkey. This bird is very mild tasting so a variety of interesting marinades, rubs, brushing sauces, and toppings can make it into a special dish.

Makes 12 servings

Thyme Marinade

- ¼ cup canola oil
- ¼ cup dry white wine
- 2 cloves garlic, minced
- 2 tablespoons crushed black peppercorns
- 1 teaspoon fresh thyme, *or* ½ teaspoon dried

Sun-Dried Tomato Dust

- ½ cup sun-dried tomatoes
- ¼ cup dried shiitake mushrooms
- ½ teaspoon black peppercorns

Turkey

- 6 lbs. turkey breast, bone in, skin discarded, wash turkey and pat dry
- 3–4 handfuls hickory or mesquite chips, soaked in water 30 minutes, drained

Thyme Marinade: Combine all ingredients in small glass bowl. Put turkey in plastic bag. Pour marinade over turkey breast and seal bag securely. Turn bag several times so that all sides of turkey are touched by marinade. Put bag in large bowl and refrigerate 6 to 8 hours or as long as overnight. Turn bag several times during marinating process.

Sun-Dried Tomato Dust: To make "dust" you further dry out already dried vegetables, in this case sun-dried tomatoes and dried shiitake mushrooms. Preheat oven to 225°. Tear tomatoes apart and discard seeds. Break off and discard mushroom stems. Arrange tomatoes and mushrooms on baking sheet. Bake vegetables in center of oven 40 minutes or until crisp but not burned. Tomatoes will dry in about 40 minutes but mushrooms take about 1 hour.

Puree vegetables in food processor along with peppercorns until all is a fine dust. Let dust settle a few minutes, then remove and store in shallow bowl, covered.

Turkey: Rub dust over turkey breast.

Prepare smoker according to manufacturer's directions. Fill fire pan about three-quarters full of hardwood charcoal and heat coals until hot.

Arrange drained chips over hot coals. Fill water pan of smoker about three-quarters full with hot water and set in place in smoker.

Place turkey breast on upper grid in smoker and cover. Smoke turkey breast about 5 hours, until internal temperature reaches 160° and juices run clear when tip of knife is inserted. Again, remember that cooking time varies depending on thickness of food and heat from coals.

While smoking, remember not to remove lid of smoker more than is necessary because it allows heat and moisture to escape, which slows the smoking process. While using the smoker, check every 30 minutes to see if hot water or coals have to be replenished; be careful and use pot holders.

Remove turkey and let stand 10 minutes before slicing. Good hot or cold. Smoked turkey is excellent with hot couscous or rice.

Nutritional Data

PER SERVING		EXCHANGES	
Calories	202	Milk	0.0
% Calories from fat	24	Veg.	0.5
Fat (gm)	5.2	Fruit	0.0
Sat. Fat (gm)	1.3	Bread	0.0
Cholesterol (mg)	78.3	Meat	3.5
Sodium (mg)	119	Fat	0.0
Protein (gm)	34.3		
Carbohydrate (gm)	2.5		

TURKEY BREAST WITH GEORGIA PEACH MOP

Try 2 oranges sliced thin and placed in the hot water pan of the smoker for an aromatic.

Makes 12 servings

Orange Marinade
- ¾ cup orange juice
- ¼ cup canola oil
- ¼ cup orange, *or* peach all fruit preserves
- ¼ cup red wine vinegar
- ½ teaspoon garlic powder

Georgia Peach Mopping Sauce
- 1 cup canned crushed tomatoes and juice
- 1 large peach, peeled, pit discarded
- 1 tablespoon fresh lime juice
- 1 tablespoon brown sugar
- ½ teaspoon ground cinnamon
- Dash red pepper flakes

Turkey
- 6 lbs. turkey breast, bone in, skin discarded, wash turkey and pat dry
- 3–4 handfuls hickory chips, soaked in water 30 minutes, drained

Orange Marinade: In a small glass bowl, whisk together all ingredients. Place turkey breast in plastic bag and add marinade. Seal bag securely and turn it several times so that all surfaces of the turkey breast touch the marinade. Place bag in bowl and put in refrigerator to marinate 6 to 8 hours or as long as overnight. Turn several times while turkey is marinating. Drain before using.

Georgia Peach Mopping Sauce: Puree tomatoes with juice, peach, lime juice, sugar, cinnamon, and pepper flakes using a food processor or blender.

Prepare smoker according to manufacturer's directions. Fill fire pan about three-quarters full of hardwood charcoal and heat coals until hot. Arrange drained chips over hot coals. Fill water pan of smoker about three-quarters full with hot water. Add orange slices if desired. Set pan in place in smoker.

Turkey: Brush thoroughly with peach mopping sauce and place turkey on upper grid of smoker. Cover smoker and cook turkey breast about 5 hours or until internal temperature reaches 160°. Turkey is done when juices run clear when pierced with tip of knife.

While smoking, remember not to remove lid of smoker more than is necessary because it allows heat and moisture to escape, which slows the smoking process. But each time you remove cover, mop turkey breast quickly. Also, while using smoker, check every 30 minutes to see if hot water or coals have to be replenished; be careful and use pot holders.

Let turkey rest 10 minutes before slicing. Serve hot or cold.

Nutritional Data

PER SERVING		EXCHANGES	
Calories	211	Milk	0.0
% Calories from fat	23	Veg.	0.0
Fat (gm)	5.2	Fruit	0.5
Sat. Fat (gm)	1.3	Bread	0.0
Cholesterol (mg)	78.3	Meat	3.5
Sodium (mg)	105	Fat	0.0
Protein (gm)	34.1		
Carbohydrate (gm)	5.2		

SMOKED TURKEY SAUSAGES WITH CARAMELIZED ONIONS

You can use aromatics of your choice in the smoker's water pan. Examples are slices of lime, lemon, or orange, cinnamon sticks, allspice, apples, and ginger.

Makes 6 servings

6 turkey sausages, spiced, available at supermarkets
1 teaspoon olive oil
2 large Vidalia onions, *or* other sweet onions, sliced
4 cloves garlic, minced
½ cup, packed, light brown sugar
¼ teaspoon each ingredient: salt and pepper
2 teaspoons celery seeds
1 can (16 ozs.) sauerkraut, drained

Prepare smoker according to manufacturer's directions. Fill fire pan about three-quarters full of hardwood charcoal and heat coals. Fill water pan about three-quarters full with hot water.

Prick sausages with fork about three times. Place sausages on top grid and cover smoker quickly. Smoke sausages about 45 minutes.

While sausages are smoking, prepare the onions. Heat oil in non-stick frying pan. Add onions and garlic and sauté over medium heat, covered, 5 minutes; stir once or twice as needed. Remove cover and add sugar, salt, and pepper. Continue cooking 5 minutes or until onions are caramelized, a light golden color. Sprinkle with celery seeds. Reheat to serve.

Sausages will turn a golden color and should be cooked through. Remove sausages to individual plates. Serve with onions, sauerkraut, and dark bread (optional).

Nutritional Data

PER SERVING		EXCHANGES	
Calories	181	Milk	0.0
% Calories from fat	29	Veg.	2.0
Fat (gm)	6.1	Fruit	0.0
Sat. Fat (gm)	0.9	Bread	1.0
Cholesterol (mg)	23	Meat	0.5
Sodium (mg)	794	Fat	0.5
Protein (gm)	6.1		
Carbohydrate (gm)	27.2		

LIME-GINGER SMOKED SALMON

A perfect way to store fresh ginger is to peel it, place it in a small jar, cover it with sherry, and refrigerate. The sherry adds flavor and body to the taste of the ginger.

Makes 6 servings

1 whole salmon, about 3 lbs., cleaned, head discarded
  Juice of 1 lime
1 tablespoon grated lime peel
1 tablespoon fresh ginger, peeled, cut into very thin slices
1 teaspoon powdered ginger
3 handfuls dried apple or maple twigs, soaked in water 30 minutes, drained
1 can (12 ozs.) apple juice (to put in water pan for aromatic)
½ teaspoon powdered ginger, *or* 3 slices (thickness of a quarter) fresh ginger
3 cups cooked brown rice, *or* couscous

W ash and pat salmon dry. Rub salmon with lime juice. Put ginger slices and lime peel inside cavity of fish. Sprinkle powdered ginger over exterior of fish. Cover fish lightly with plastic wrap and refrigerate 2 hours.

Prepare smoker according to manufacturer's directions. Fill fire pan about three-quarters full of hardwood charcoal and heat coals until hot. Arrange twigs over hot coals. Fill water pan about three-quarters full with hot water. Add apple juice and ginger to water pan and place pan in smoker as aromatic.

Unwrap salmon and place on sprayed grid. Cover quickly. Smoke salmon about 3 hours or until fish flakes easily when prodded with fork. Skin will turn a smoky color.

While smoking, remember not to remove lid of smoker more than is necessary because it allows heat and moisture to escape, which slows the smoking process. Also, while using smoker, check every 30 minutes to see if hot water or coals have to be replenished. Be careful and use pot holders.

Serve fish warm or cold with hot rice.

Nutritional Data

PER SERVING		EXCHANGES	
Calories	318	Milk	0.0
% Calories from fat	25	Veg.	0.0
Fat (gm)	8.6	Fruit	0.0
Sat. Fat (gm)	1.8	Bread	1.5
Cholesterol (mg)	40.7	Meat	4.0
Sodium (mg)	141	Fat	0.0
Protein (gm)	34.9		
Carbohydrate (gm)	23.2		

SMOKED WHITEFISH WITH HERB DRESSING

Whitefish is from the Great Lakes. Substitutes for this medium-flavored fish can be salmon or haddock. Both fillets and the whole fish work well on smoker or grill.

Makes 4 servings

4 small whitefish, about 6 ozs. each, cleaned, scaled, head and tail intact

2 oranges, sliced

3 handfuls cherry or other fruit wood chips (optional), soaked in water 30 minutes, drained

Garden Herb Dressing

¾ cup plain non-fat yogurt

½ cup fat-free mayonnaise

3 tablespoons minced parsley

1½ teaspoons minced basil

¾ teaspoon minced tarragon

⅓ teaspoon pepper

Wash and pat dry the whitefish. Place orange slices in fish cavities.

Prepare smoker according to manufacturer's directions. Fill fire pan about three-quarters full of hardwood charcoal and heat coals until hot. Arrange drained wood chips over hot coals. Fill water pan of smoker about three-quarters full with hot water and place in smoker. You may want to add 1 slice of orange to the water for aromatic effect.

Place fish on grid, cover, and smoke fish 45 minutes to 1 hour or until cooked (fish will flake easily when prodded with fork and skin will be a golden smoky color).

Garden Herb Dressing: While fish are smoking, prepare dressing. In a small bowl, mix together yogurt and mayonnaise. Stir in herbs and pepper. Taste to adjust flavors.

To serve, place 1 fish on each plate, with dressing on the side. Good warm or cold.

Nutritional Data

PER SERVING		EXCHANGES	
Calories	311	Milk	0.0
% Calories from fat	30	Veg.	0.0
Fat (gm)	10.2	Fruit	0.5
Sat. Fat (gm)	1.6	Bread	0.5
Cholesterol (mg)	102.9	Meat	4.5
Sodium (mg)	501	Fat	0.0
Protein (gm)	35.8		
Carbohydrate (gm)	17.7		

HICKORY-SMOKED SHRIMP DIP WITH CRUDITÉS

Makes 6 servings

Chili Mopping Sauce
- ⅓ cup chili sauce
- 2 teaspoons chili powder
- ½ teaspoon cumin seeds

Shrimp Dip
- ¾ lb. large shrimp, peeled, deveined, washed, patted dry
- Non-stick cooking spray
- 3–4 handfuls hickory chips, soaked in water 30 minutes, drained
- ½ lb. 1% small-curd cottage cheese
- ½ lb. part-skim ricotta cheese
- ¼ cup plain non-fat yogurt
- ¼ cup minced onion
- ¼ teaspoon each ingredient: garlic powder, salt, pepper

Vegetable Crudités
- 1 red or green bell pepper, seeded, sliced
- 2 stalks celery, cut lengthwise, and cut again into 4-in. pieces
- 3 carrots, cut lengthwise and cut again into 4-in. pieces

P repare smoker according to manufacturer's directions. Fill fire pan about three-quarters full of hardwood charcoal and heat coals until hot. Arrange drained hickory chips over hot coals. Fill water pan of smoker about three-quarters full with hot water and set pan in place in smoker.

Chili Mopping Sauce: Combine ingredients in small glass bowl. Mop shrimp thoroughly.

Shrimp Dip: Place shrimp on sprayed grill rack placed on grid of smoker. Smoke shrimp 25 to 30 minutes. Shrimp look opaque when done and lose their translucent appearance. Chop shrimp into small pieces and set aside.

While shrimp are smoking, mix together cheeses, yogurt, onions, garlic powder, salt, and pepper. Mix in chopped shrimp. Transfer dip to a serving bowl, cover, and refrigerate until ready to serve. Before serving, mix again and taste to adjust seasonings.

Vegetable Crudités: Cut up vegetables and arrange them decoratively on a platter. Cover loosely with plastic wrap and refrigerate until ready to serve. Use crudités to scoop up shrimp dip.

Nutritional Data

PER SERVING		EXCHANGES	
Calories	167	Milk	0.0
% Calories from fat	23	Veg.	1.0
Fat (gm)	4.2	Fruit	0.0
Sat. Fat (gm)	2.3	Bread	0.0
Cholesterol (mg)	101	Meat	2.5
Sodium (mg)	564	Fat	0.0
Protein (gm)	12		
Carbohydrate (gm)	12.4		

SMOKED MUSSELS WITH CAPONATA RELISH

Makes 4 servings

Caponata Relish (recipe follows)
48 green-lip mussels, *or* mussels of your choice, scrubbed, debearded
3–4 handfuls alderwood or hickory chips, soaked in water 30 minutes, drained
1 green bell pepper (for Caponata Relish)
1 tomato (for Caponata Relish)

Prepare smoker according to manufacturer's directions. Fill fire pan about three-quarters full of hardwood charcoal and heat coals until hot. Arrange drained wood chips over hot coals. Fill water pan of smoker about three-quarters full with hot water and set pan in place in smoker.

Place mussels on grid and cover smoker. Put pepper and tomato on grid to smoke vegetables with mussels. Smoke mussels 6 to 10 minutes. Mussels should open; discard any unopened mussels. Reserve pepper and tomato for caponata.

Place mussels on individual plates and serve with caponata relish.

Caponata Relish

1 teaspoon olive oil
3 cloves garlic, minced
½ cup minced onion
1 cup peeled, diced eggplant
1 smoked green bell pepper, seeded, chopped
1 smoked tomato, peeled, chopped
2 tablespoons capers
1 teaspoon red wine vinegar

Heat oil in non-stick saucepan. Sauté garlic and onions, covered, over medium heat 4 to 5 minutes or until tender. Stir as needed. Add eggplant and stir to combine. Sauté 4 minutes or until eggplant is soft; it will brown slightly. Add peppers, tomato, capers, and vinegar. Continue cooking 5 minutes. Taste to adjust seasonings.

Spoon caponata into a bowl and serve with mussels.

Nutritional Data

PER SERVING		EXCHANGES	
Calories	244	Milk	0.0
% Calories from fat	24	Veg.	3.0
Fat (gm)	6.5	Fruit	0.0
Sat. Fat (gm)	1.2	Bread	0.0
Cholesterol (mg)	64	Meat	3.0
Sodium (mg)	504	Fat	0.0
Protein (gm)	28		
Carbohydrate (gm)	17.4		

BARBECUE PORK SANDWICH WITH WHISKEY-BAKED BEANS

Most of the southern regions have a local version of the barbecued sandwich. You can adjust the mop sauce to your taste, that is, you can make it spicy or sweet. With the beans, these sandwiches make an entire meal.

Makes 6 servings

Whiskey-Baked Beans (recipe follows)

Tomato Mopping Sauce

    Non-stick cooking spray

- ½ cup minced onion
- ¼ cup ketchup
- 2 medium tomatoes, peeled, seeded, chopped
- 2 tablespoons whiskey
- 2 teaspoons chili powder
- ½ teaspoon ground cumin
    Dash Tabasco sauce
- ¼ cup, packed, dark brown sugar
- 1 tablespoon fresh lime, *or* lemon juice
- ½ cup tomato juice
- 3–4 handfuls mesquite chips, soaked in water 30 minutes, drained

Pork

- 1½ lbs. boneless pork loin, trimmed of fat
- 3 French bread rolls, cut in half, lightly toasted

Tomato Mopping Sauce: Heat a sprayed non-stick small saucepan over medium heat. Sauté onion, covered, about 4 minutes, stirring as necessary. Blend in remaining ingredients. Bring mixture to a boil, reduce heat, and continue simmering 5 minutes. Cool. Puree sauce in food processor or blender.

Prepare smoker according to manufacturer's directions. Fill fire pan about three-quarters full of hardwood charcoal and heat coals until hot. Arrange drained mesquite chips over hot coals. Fill water pan of smoker about three-quarters full with hot water and set pan in place in smoker.

Pork: Brush pork liberally with mopping sauce. Place pork on top grid, cover, and smoke loin about 1½ hours or until pork is no longer pink in center. Brush pork once or twice with sauce during smoking.

While smoking, remember not to remove lid of smoker more than is necessary because it allows heat and moisture to escape, which slows the smoking process. Also, check smoker every 30 minutes to see if hot water or coals have to be replenished. Be careful and use pot holders.

Remove pork to cutting board and let stand 5 minutes. Brush generously with remaining sauce. Shred pork with sharp knife. Spoon pork onto halves of French rolls and serve with whiskey-baked beans.

Whiskey-Baked Beans

- 1 lb. dry pinto beans, wash and discard pieces or shriveled beans
- 1 cup chopped onion
- ½ cup molasses
- 2 tablespoons dark brown sugar
- ¼ cup ketchup
- ½ teaspoon ground ginger
- ½ teaspoon salt
- ¼ teaspoon pepper
- 2 tablespoons whiskey

Put beans and onions in large, heavy pot and fill pot half-way with water. Bring mixture to a boil over medium heat. Reduce heat to simmer and cover. Continue cooking until beans are tender, about 3 hours. Add hot water as necessary to keep beans covered. Cool and drain beans but reserve liquid.

Preheat oven to 300°. Place beans in bean pot, if available, or in heavy pot with lid. Mix in molasses, sugar, ketchup, ginger, salt, and pepper. Stir in only enough of reserved bean liquid to cover beans. Cover and bake 2½ to 3 hours, stirring beans every 30 minutes. Remove cover during last hour of baking. Mix in whiskey to taste. Serve beans hot. Beans can be prepared 2 or 3 days in advance and reheated to serve.

Nutritional Data

PER SERVING		EXCHANGES	
Calories	635	Milk	0.0
% Calories from fat	14	Veg.	1.0
Fat (gm)	9.9	Fruit	0.0
Sat. Fat (gm)	3	Bread	6.0
Cholesterol (mg)	51	Meat	2.5
Sodium (mg)	764	Fat	0.5
Protein (gm)	34.3		
Carbohydrate (gm)	99.9		

Smoked Southwest Back Ribs with Refried Beans

Like the preceding recipe, the ribs and beans comprise a one-dish meal that's convenient and flavorful.

Makes 8 servings

Tomato-Beer Mopping Sauce

Non-stick cooking spray
- 3 cloves garlic
- ½ cup minced onion
- ¾ cup beer
- ¼ cup red wine vinegar
- ⅓ cup ketchup
- 1 cup tomato juice
- 1 teaspoon Worcestershire sauce
- 2 tablespoons dark brown sugar
- 1½ teaspoons chili powder
- ¾ teaspoon ground cumin
- ¼ teaspoon pepper

Ribs
- 3 lbs. baby back ribs, in slabs, discard visible fat
- 3–4 handfuls mesquite chips, soaked in water 30 minutes, drained

Refried Beans
- 2 cans (15 ozs. each) black beans, drained, reserve liquid
- ½ cup chopped onion
- 1 teaspoon chili powder
- 1 teaspoon cumin seeds
- ¼ teaspoon pepper
  Dash hot sauce
- ¼ cup chopped cilantro

Tomato-Beer Mopping Sauce: Heat sprayed non-stick saucepan. Sauté garlic and onions, covered, over medium heat 4 to 5 minutes or until tender. Stir as necessary. Stir in remaining sauce ingredients. Reduce heat to simmer and cook 5 minutes, uncovered. Stir once or twice. Cool. Mopping sauce can be made day before serving.

Ribs: Add water to large pot or kettle and bring to a boil. Add steamer rack, making sure it rises above water level. Reduce heat to simmer. Add ribs and cover tightly. Steam ribs to precook them and render fat. Steam 20 minutes or until ribs are partially cooked. Cool.

Transfer ribs to glass dish and mop amply on both sides. Let ribs stand at room temperature 1 hour.

Meanwhile, prepare smoker according to manufacturer's directions. Fill fire pan about three-quarters full of hardwood charcoal and heat coals until hot. Arrange mesquite chips over hot coals. Fill water pan of smoker two-thirds full with hot water and place in smoker.

Mop ribs again with sauce and place on sprayed grid. Cover smoker. Cook ribs about 1 hour until tender. Smoking time depends on thickness of ribs and heat of coals. Check every 30 minutes to see if hot water or coals have to be replenished. Be careful and use pot holders.

Refried Beans: While ribs are smoking, drain and mash beans. Heat a sprayed non-stick frying pan over medium heat. Sauté onions over medium heat, covered, 4 to 5 minutes or until tender. Add beans, chili powder, cumin seeds, pepper, and hot sauce. Continue cooking and stirring as necessary until beans are hot. Add reserved liquid if beans become too dry. Serve beans sprinkled with cilantro.

Transfer rib slabs to cutting board and slice into single ribs. Divide ribs among individual plates and serve hot with refried beans.

Nutritional Data

PER SERVING		EXCHANGES	
Calories	437	Milk	0.0
% Calories from fat	36	Veg.	0.6
Fat (gm)	18.4	Fruit	0.0
Sat. Fat (gm)	7.2	Bread	1.4
Cholesterol (mg)	100	Meat	4.4
Sodium (mg)	688	Fat	0.5
Protein (gm)	43.4		
Carbohydrate (gm)	29.9		

PECOS RIVER BEEF BRISKET WITH BARBECUE SAUCE AND RICE

Makes 10 servings

3 lbs. beef brisket, all visible fat cut off

Brown Sugar Barbecue Sauce

Non-stick cooking spray

¼ cup minced onion

3 cloves garlic

½ cup ketchup

¼ cup water

3 tablespoons cider vinegar

3 tablespoons fresh orange juice

3 tablespoons fresh lime juice

3 tablespoons dark brown sugar

1½ teaspoons chili powder

½ teaspoon Worcestershire sauce

½ teaspoon celery seeds

¼ teaspoon each ingredient: salt, Tabasco sauce, pepper

3–4 cups hickory chips, soaked in water 30 minutes, drained

½ cup cumin seeds (optional) for aromatic in water pan

8 cups cooked brown rice

½ cup chopped cilantro, *or* parsley

Put brisket in large pan, cover with water, and simmer 2 hours. Drain.

Barbecue Sauce: While brisket is simmering, prepare barbecue sauce. Heat a sprayed non-stick saucepan and sauté onions and garlic, covered, over medium heat for a few minutes until onions are tender. Stir onions as necessary. Add remaining sauce ingredients and simmer, uncovered, 5 minutes, stirring occasionally. Cool sauce. Makes 1½ cups.

Prepare smoker according to manufacturer's directions. Fill fire pan about three-quarters full of hardwood charcoal and heat coals until hot. Arrange hickory chips over hot coals. Fill water pan of smoker about three-quarters full with hot water. Add cumin seeds. Set water pan in place.

Brush brisket amply with barbecue sauce, wrap it in double thickness of aluminum foil, and arrange it in center of top smoker grid.

Cover smoker and cook about 2 hours. Brisket should be fork-tender. Check every 30 minutes to see if coals or water need to be replaced in smoker. Mop brisket with sauce when you check.

Transfer brisket to cutting board and cool 10 minutes. Cut into thin slices against the grain. Toss rice with cilantro and serve with the meat.

Nutritional Data

PER SERVING		EXCHANGES	
Calories	454	Milk	0.0
% Calories from fat	29	Veg.	0.0
Fat (gm)	14.5	Fruit	0.0
Sat. Fat (gm)	4.9	Bread	3.0
Cholesterol (mg)	94	Meat	4.0
Sodium (mg)	305	Fat	0.5
Protein (gm)	34.2		
Carbohydrate (gm)	45.8		

8.
WOK GRILLING

Stir-Fried Beef with Tomatoes, Peppers, Oyster Sauce, and Rice

Hot and Spicy Chicken

Chicken with Hoisin Sauce and Rice

Stir-Fried Turkey Sausage and Penne

Stir-Fried Pork, Onions, and Noodles

Spiked Broccoli with Shrimp and Rice

Stir-Fry Vegetables

Stir-Fried Asparagus, Green Beans, and 2 Mushrooms

Stir-Fried Snow Peas, Peppers, and Green Onions with Rice

Sliced Cucumber Salad

Why not use a wok on the grill? After all, the wok was originally designed to be used on an outdoor fire. Try it and you'll find that this method of stir-frying on a grill adds to the versatility of outdoor cooking. You can wok cook all or part of the meal on the grill. For example, one can grill chicken breasts and then quickly stir-fry a vegetable dish to serve along with the chicken.

For best results, use a flat-bottomed wok, or if you are using a round-bottomed wok, use the wok ring or remove the grill's grid and fit the wok evenly onto the coals.

STIR-FRIED BEEF WITH TOMATOES, PEPPERS, OYSTER SAUCE, AND RICE

Makes 4 Servings

Oyster Sauce
- 3 tablespoons reduced-sodium soy sauce
- 3 tablespoons dry white wine
- 1 teaspoon sugar
- 1 tablespoon cornstarch, mixed with 2 tablespoons water
- 1 tablespoon oyster sauce

Stir-Fry
- Non-stick cooking spray
- 4 green onions, trimmed, cut in halves lengthwise, and cut again into 1½-in. strips
- 3 cloves garlic, minced
- 1 teaspoon minced ginger
- ¾ lb. flank steak, chilled for easy slicing, cut against the grain into thin slices about ⅛ in. thick, and cut again into 1½-in. pieces
- 1 large red or green bell pepper, seeded, sliced
- 1 cup tomato wedges

- 4 cups cooked brown, *or* white, rice

Oyster Sauce: Combine ingredients in a small bowl. Have sauce handy, next to the grill.

Stir-Fry: Cut and prepare meat and vegetables. Have them ready, next to the wok.

In a sprayed non-stick or regular wok on grid over ashen-hot coals, quickly stir-fry onions, garlic, and ginger about 1 minute. Have a glass of water or defatted beef stock handy to add to wok if it gets too dry. Stir in ¼ cup water or stock as needed. Add meat pieces and stir-fry 2 to 5 minutes until meat loses its color. Add tomatoes and pepper; cook only until they are heated. Stir in sauce. Stir-fry until all food is coated with sauce, 1 or 2 minutes.

Remove wok from grill using pot holders, as it can be very hot. Serve stir-fry food with hot rice in individual bowls.

Nutritional Data

PER SERVING		EXCHANGES	
Calories	406	Milk	0.0
% Calories from fat	17	Veg.	1.0
Fat (gm)	7.6	Fruit	0.0
Sat. Fat (gm)	2.8	Bread	3.0
Cholesterol (mg)	35	Meat	3.0
Sodium (mg)	585	Fat	0.0
Protein (gm)	27.7		
Carbohydrate (gm)	54		

HOT AND SPICY CHICKEN

Remember that stir-fry time is very short; the essence of this type of cookery is to cook the food quickly over high heat. Have all ingredients nearby while cooking. Keep a glass of water or defatted chicken stock handy in case the wok becomes too dry. Add ¼ cup of the water or stock at a time.

Makes 4 servings

Sauce

- ¼ cup fat-free chicken stock
- 1 tablespoon cornstarch mixed with 2 tablespoons water, *or* chicken stock
- 3 tablespoons reduced-sodium soy sauce
- 2 tablespoons rice wine
- 2 teaspoons sugar
- ½ teaspoon oriental sesame seed oil

Stir-Fry

- ¾ lb. chicken breast pieces, boned, skinned, cut into 1-in. pieces
- 1 egg white
- 1 tablespoon cornstarch
  Non-stick cooking spray
- 4 green onions, cut in halves lengthwise, and cut again into 1½-in. pieces
- ¼ cup fat-free chicken stock
- 2 cloves garlic, minced
- 1 green bell pepper, seeded, cut into thin strips
- ½ cup sliced bamboo shoots, rinsed, drained

- 4 teaspoons unsalted roasted peanuts (optional)
- 4 cups cooked brown, *or* white, rice

Sauce: Mix ingredients in a small glass bowl. Have sauce and small glass of water or chicken stock handy as you cook.

Toss chicken with egg white mixed with cornstarch. Set aside.

Stir-Fry: In a sprayed non-stick or regular wok on grid over ashen-hot coals, stir-fry onions with chicken stock and garlic about 1 minute. Add chicken and stir-fry 2 to 5 minutes until cooked. Add pepper strips and bamboo shoots. Stir fry until hot. Mix in sauce and cook until food is coated with sauce.

Transfer chicken to serving bowl, sprinkle with peanuts (optional), and serve hot with rice.

Nutritional Data

PER SERVING		EXCHANGES	
Calories	344	Milk	0.0
% Calories from fat	11	Veg.	1.0
Fat (gm)	4	Fruit	0.0
Sat. Fat (gm)	0.9	Bread	3.0
Cholesterol (mg)	34	Meat	2.0
Sodium (mg)	493	Fat	0.0
Protein (gm)	21		
Carbohydrate (gm)	54.6		

CHICKEN WITH HOISIN SAUCE AND RICE

Hoisin sauce is full bodied, rich, and bean-based. It is available at oriental food stores and large supermarkets. When my daughter was young, she preferred it to ketchup. As a matter of fact, I think she still does.

Makes 4 servings

Hoisin Sauce

- 3 tablespoons hoisin sauce
- 1 teaspoon sugar
- ½ cup fat-free chicken stock, *or* water

Stir-Fry

- Non-stick cooking spray
- 1 lb. chicken breast, skin and bones discarded
- 1 egg white
- 2 tablespoons cornstarch
- 3 green onions, cut in halves lengthwise, and cut again into ½-in. pieces
- 2 cloves garlic, minced
- ½ teaspoon grated ginger
- ¼ cup fat-free chicken stock
- 2 cups shredded bok choy, *or* sliced celery
- 1 red bell pepper, seeded, sliced thin
- ¼ teaspoon each ingredient: salt and pepper

- 3 cups cooked brown, *or* white, rice

Hoisin Sauce: Combine hoisin sauce, sugar, and chicken stock in a small glass bowl. Have sauce readily available next to the grill.

Toss chicken with egg white mixed with cornstarch. Set aside.

Stir-Fry: In a sprayed non-stick or regular wok on grid over ashen-hot coals, stir-fry onions, garlic, and ginger about 1 minute. Add chicken and stir-fry until cooked, 2 to 5 minutes. If chicken sticks to bottom of wok, stir in stock. Add bok choy, bell pepper, salt, and pepper. Stir-fry only until food is hot; do not overcook. Stir in sauce.

Remove wok from grill using pot holders. Spoon food into a serving bowl, and serve hot with rice.

Nutritional Data

PER SERVING		EXCHANGES	
Calories	308	Milk	0.0
% Calories from fat	11	Veg.	1.0
Fat (gm)	3.6	Fruit	0.0
Sat. Fat (gm)	0.8	Bread	2.5
Cholesterol (mg)	46	Meat	2.0
Sodium (mg)	416	Fat	0.0
Protein (gm)	23.6		
Carbohydrate (gm)	44.8		

STIR-FRIED TURKEY SAUSAGE AND PENNE

Makes 4 servings

Non-stick cooking spray
1 teaspoon olive oil
3 cloves garlic, minced
1 cup sliced onion
¾ lb. Italian-flavored turkey sausage cut into
   ½-in. pieces
1 large red bell pepper, seeded, sliced thin
¾ cup grated carrots
1 can (14½ ozs.) sliced tomatoes, include juice
1 teaspoon oregano
¾ teaspoon basil
¼ teaspoon each ingredient: salt and pepper
3 cups penne pasta, cooked according to pkg.
   directions, drained

Have all ingredients near grill for fast, easy preparation. Set sprayed non-stick or regular wok on grid over ashen-hot coals.

To wok, add oil, garlic, and onions. Stir-fry about 1 minute. Add sausage and continue stir-frying 2 to 5 minutes or until cooked. Add pepper, carrots, tomatoes with juice, and spices. Stir-fry only until hot. Mix in pasta.

Remove wok from grill using pot holders, and serve this one-dish meal.

Nutritional Data

PER SERVING		EXCHANGES	
Calories	323	Milk	0.0
% Calories from fat	28	Veg.	2.0
Fat (gm)	10.3	Fruit	0.0
Sat. Fat (gm)	1.9	Bread	2.0
Cholesterol (mg)	50	Meat	2.0
Sodium (mg)	752	Fat	0.5
Protein (gm)	18.7		
Carbohydrate (gm)	42.1		

STIR-FRIED PORK, ONIONS, AND NOODLES

*This dish has the noodles cooked in the wok.
It is a one-dish meal.*

Makes 4 servings

Sauce

- ½ cup fat-free chicken stock
- 1 tablespoon cornstarch mixed with 2 tablespoons chicken stock, *or* water
- 2 tablespoons low-sodium soy sauce
- 1 teaspoon grated orange rind
- ½ teaspoon oriental sesame seed oil
- ¼ teaspoon pepper

Stir-Fry

- Non-stick cooking spray
- 2 cups sliced onion
- ¼ cup fat-free chicken stock
- 4 cloves garlic, minced
- 1 teaspoon minced ginger
- ¾ lb. pork tenderloin, chilled about 30 minutes in freezer for easy, thin slicing
- 1 cup sliced mushrooms
- 2 cups cooked oriental noodles, *or* spaghetti, first broken into 4-in. pieces, cooked according to pkg. directions

Sauce: Mix all ingredients in a small glass bowl. Place near grill so that it is handy for cooking.

Stir-Fry: Set sprayed non-stick or regular wok on grid over ashen-hot coals. Stir-fry onions, adding stock as necessary if onions stick to wok. Add garlic and ginger and mix well. Add pork and mushrooms and continue stir-frying 2 to 5 minutes or until pork is cooked. Mix in sauce and noodles. Cook until hot, only a minute or two.

Remove wok from grill using pot holders. Divide food into individual plates and serve hot.

Nutritional Data

PER SERVING		EXCHANGES	
Calories	227	Milk	0.0
% Calories from fat	16	Veg.	2.0
Fat (gm)	4.2	Fruit	0.0
Sat. Fat (gm)	1.2	Bread	1.0
Cholesterol (mg)	60	Meat	2.0
Sodium (mg)	409	Fat	0.0
Protein (gm)	24.8		
Carbohydrate (gm)	23.7		

Spiked Broccoli with Shrimp and Rice

The broccoli in this recipe is lightly flavored with gin. You can substitute wine, or if you like, omit the alcohol altogether.

Makes 4 servings

- 1 lb. broccoli, cut florets, and cut stems into ¼-in. rounds
- 1 teaspoon canola oil
- 2 cloves garlic, minced
- 1 teaspoon grated ginger
- ¾ lb. extra-large shrimp, peeled, deveined, washed, patted dry
- 3 tablespoons gin, *or* dry white wine
- 2 tablespoons dark brown sugar
- 2 tablespoons low-sodium soy sauce
- 3 cups cooked brown, *or* white rice, *or* oriental noodles, served hot

Blanch broccoli by bringing lightly salted water to a boil, adding broccoli, and cooking 2 minutes. Drain.

Set non-stick or regular wok on grid over ashen-hot coals. Add oil, garlic, and ginger and stir-fry 1 minute. Add broccoli, cover, and cook 2 to 3 minutes, removing cover and stirring once or twice so broccoli does not stick to bottom of wok.

Remove cover and add shrimp; stir-fry until shrimp are cooked. Do not overcook shrimp; they are done when they turn pinkish white from their natural opaque color.

Stir in gin, brown sugar, and soy sauce. Serve with hot rice.

Nutritional Data

PER SERVING		EXCHANGES	
Calories	327	Milk	0.0
% Calories from fat	9	Veg.	2.5
Fat (gm)	3.3	Fruit	0.0
Sat. Fat (gm)	0.6	Bread	2.5
Cholesterol (mg)	131	Meat	1.5
Sodium (mg)	451	Fat	0.0
Protein (gm)	22.1		
Carbohydrate (gm)	47.4		

STIR-FRY VEGETABLES

In the fall try this stir-fry with root vegetables: thin slices of potatoes, sliced carrots, onions, and garlic.

Makes 4 servings

  1 teaspoon canola oil
  3 cloves garlic, minced
  ¾ cup sliced red onion
  ½ lb. broccoli, cut florets into pieces, and cut stems into ¼-in. rounds
  1 cup sliced celery
  1 red bell pepper, seeded, cut into thin strips
  ½ cup sliced water chestnuts
  1 cup defrosted corn niblets
  2 teaspoons basil
  ¼ teaspoon each ingredient: salt and pepper
  2 tablespoons low-sodium soy sauce

Blanch broccoli by bringing lightly salted water to a boil, adding broccoli, and cooking 2 minutes. Drain.

Set non-stick or regular wok on grid over ashen-hot coals. Add oil, garlic, and onions. Stir-fry about 1 minute. If onions begin to stick, add ¼ cup water or vegetable or chicken stock. Add broccoli, cover, and cook 2 to 3 minutes, removing cover and stirring once or twice so broccoli does not stick to bottom of wok.

Remove cover and add remaining ingredients. Stir-fry only until vegetables are hot; do not overcook. Remove wok from grill using pot holders and serve.

Nutritional Data

PER SERVING		EXCHANGES	
Calories	100	Milk	0.0
% Calories from fat	11	Veg.	4.0
Fat (gm)	1.4	Fruit	0.0
Sat. Fat (gm)	0.1	Bread	0.0
Cholesterol (mg)	0	Meat	0.0
Sodium (mg)	442	Fat	0.0
Protein (gm)	4.9		
Carbohydrate (gm)	20.3		

STIR-FRIED ASPARAGUS, GREEN BEANS, AND 2 MUSHROOMS

Feel free to interchange the vegetables according to availability and personal preference. Both wild and cultivated mushrooms cook very well in a wok and can change the flavors of a dish by adding depth and taste.

Makes 4 servings

Sauce

- ¼ cup fat-free chicken, *or* vegetable stock
- 1 tablespoon cornstarch mixed with ¼ cup of chicken stock
- 1 teaspoon sugar
- 2 tablespoons low-sodium soy sauce
- 3 tablespoons dry white wine

Stir-Fry

- 1 teaspoon canola oil
- 3 cloves garlic, minced
- ½ cup red onion, sliced
- ½ lb. thin-stalked asparagus, trimmed, cut into 2-in. pieces
- ½ lb. fresh green beans, trimmed, cut in halves
- ½ lb. brown or white mushrooms, cleaned, sliced
- 1 cup fresh shiitaki mushrooms, cleaned, sliced, *or* reconstituted dry mushrooms, discard stems, slice

Sauce: Combine sauce ingredients in bowl and keep handy near grill.

Stir-Fry: Set non-stick or regular wok on grid over ashen-hot coals. Add oil, garlic, and onions. Stir-fry about 1 minute. Add asparagus and green beans and stir-fry 1 minute. Add mushrooms and sauce. Stir-fry 2 to 3 minutes or until mushrooms are cooked.

Remove wok from grill, using pot holders, and serve vegetables hot.

Nutritional Data

PER SERVING		EXCHANGES	
Calories	103	Milk	0.0
% Calories from fat	14	Veg.	2.0
Fat (gm)	1.9	Fruit	0.0
Sat. Fat (gm)	0.2	Bread	0.5
Cholesterol (mg)	0	Meat	0.0
Sodium (mg)	314	Fat	0.0
Protein (gm)	5.2		
Carbohydrate (gm)	18.1		

STIR-FRIED SNOW PEAS, PEPPERS, AND GREEN ONIONS WITH RICE

Most wok recipes can be served successfully with hot brown or white rice, oriental noodles, or spaghetti. Cook according to package directions and refresh in a colander under hot running water before serving. Salted black beans are aged soybeans that add a unique flavor. They are available in oriental food stores and are well worth the trip. Rinse and mash the beans before using.

Makes 4 servings

¾ lb. boneless, skinless chicken breast, cut into
    1-in. pieces
2 teaspoons cornstarch
1 egg white, slightly beaten
1 tablespoon canola oil
2 tablespoons fat-free chicken stock
3 cloves garlic, minced
½ teaspoon powdered ginger
1 tablespoon salted black beans, washed, put in
    small strainer and mashed with back of spoon
1 bunch green onions, trimmed, cut in halves
    lengthwise, and cut again into 1½-in. pieces
¾ lb. snow peas, trimmed
2 red bell peppers, seeded, cut into strips
3 cups cooked brown, *or* white, rice

Assemble all ingredients near the grill for fast stir-frying. Toss chicken pieces with cornstarch and egg white.

Set non-stick or regular wok on grid over ashen-hot coals. Add oil, stock, garlic, ginger powder, black beans, and chicken; stir-fry 1 to 2 minutes. Stir in green onions and stir-fry about 1 minute. Add snow peas and red peppers, and continue cooking until vegetables are tender and just heated through. Serve the stir-fry with hot rice.

Nutritional Data

PER SERVING		EXCHANGES	
Calories	323	Milk	0.0
% Calories from fat	18	Veg.	2.0
Fat (gm)	6.5	Fruit	0.0
Sat. Fat (gm)	1	Bread	2.5
Cholesterol (mg)	34	Meat	1.5
Sodium (mg)	75	Fat	0.0
Protein (gm)	20.9		
Carbohydrate (gm)	45.2		

SLICED CUCUMBER SALAD

The following recipe goes well as a side dish with many of the wok stir-fries. It can be prepared the day before serving.

Makes 4 servings

- 2 medium-large, firm cucumbers, peeled, cut in half lengthwise
- ½ cup red wine vinegar
- 2 tablespoons sugar
- ¼ teaspoon each ingredient: salt, pepper, garlic powder
- 1 cup thinly sliced Vidalia onion

Using a teaspoon, scoop out seeds of cucumber and make thin slices. Put cucumber slices in glass serving bowl. Mix in vinegar, sugar, salt, pepper, and garlic powder. Add onions and toss salad. Cover and refrigerate. Toss salad again before serving.

Nutritional Data

PER SERVING		EXCHANGES	
Calories	63	Milk	0.0
% Calories from fat	3	Veg.	2.5
Fat (gm)	0.3	Fruit	0.0
Sat. Fat (gm)	0.1	Bread	0.0
Cholesterol (mg)	0	Meat	0.0
Sodium (mg)	138	Fat	0.0
Protein (gm)	1.5		
Carbohydrate (gm)	15.6		

9.
DESSERTS

Toasted Angel Cake with Berries
◆
Angel Cake Kabobs with Chocolate Sauce
◆
Pineapple Slices with Yogurt
◆
Peach Slices with Raspberry Sauce
◆
Grilled Bananas Foster and Yogurt
◆
Grilled Figs with Vanilla-Mint Yogurt
◆
Grilled Fruit with Raspberry Sauce

TOASTED ANGEL CAKE WITH BERRIES

The following recipe is a light and easy red, white, and blue celebration of color and taste.

Makes 4 servings

4 slices angel cake, packaged
1½ cups blueberries, washed, picked over
1⅓ cups raspberries, washed, picked over
¼ cup sugar, or to taste
2 tablespoons dry white wine, *or* orange juice
1 tablespoon grated orange peel
Non-stick cooking spray

S | lice cake and have it handy at the grill.

Put blueberries, raspberries, sugar, wine, and orange peel in small saucepan. Simmer sauce about 6 minutes, stirring occasionally. Serve warm or cold.

Place sprayed grill rack on grid over ashen-hot coals. Toast cake slices and place on dessert plates. Drizzle stewed fruit over cake. You can also serve this dish with frozen strawberry or vanilla yogurt on the side.

Nutritional Data

PER SERVING		EXCHANGES	
Calories	234	Milk	0.0
% Calories from fat	2	Veg.	0.0
Fat (gm)	0.5	Fruit	1.5
Sat. Fat (gm)	0.1	Bread	2.0
Cholesterol (mg)	0	Meat	0.0
Sodium (mg)	259	Fat	0.0
Protein (gm)	3.9		
Carbohydrate (gm)	54.7		

ANGEL CAKE KABOBS WITH CHOCOLATE SAUCE

The angel cake is heated on skewers over the grill. Guests can even grill their own kabobs. Have the chocolate sauce ready to serve, and you have an easy and elegant outdoor dessert.

Makes 4 servings

Chocolate Sauce

- ½ cup sugar
- ½ cup apple juice
- 2 tablespoons cocoa
- ¼ cup water
- 2 teaspoons butter
- ½ teaspoon vanilla

Kabobs

- 4 slices packaged angel food cake, cut into 1-in. pieces
- 2 large nectarines, sliced
- 4 small double-pronged skewers, *or* bamboo skewers soaked in water briefly and drained
- Non-stick cooking spray

Chocolate Sauce: Mix together sugar, apple juice, and cocoa. Whisk in water. Bring chocolate sauce to a boil over medium-low heat. Continue cooking and whisking constantly for only 1 minute. Remove pan from heat and mix in butter and vanilla. Cool and serve sauce at room temperature.

Kabobs: Thread skewers with nectarine slices and angel food cake.

Spray a grill rack and place it on grid over ashen-hot coals. Grill kabobs about 5 minutes or until hot, turning frequently.

To serve, spoon chocolate sauce on each dessert plate. Set kabobs over sauce.

Nutritional Data

PER SERVING		EXCHANGES	
Calories	297	Milk	0.0
% Calories from fat	8	Veg.	0.0
Fat (gm)	2.6	Fruit	1.0
Sat. Fat (gm)	1.3	Bread	3.0
Cholesterol (mg)	5	Meat	0.0
Sodium (mg)	277	Fat	0.5
Protein (gm)	4.3		
Carbohydrate (gm)	67.7		

PINEAPPLE SLICES WITH YOGURT

When choosing a pineapple, do not buy one that has brown, dry leaves. You want a pineapple that is fresh looking and smells fruity. Then refrigerate the ripe fruit. Many large supermarkets sell fresh pineapple already peeled.

Makes 4 servings

4 slices fresh pineapple, cut into ½-in.-thick slices

Brown Sugar-Orange Juice Mopping Sauce

¼ cup, packed, dark brown sugar

½ teaspoon cinnamon

Dash ground nutmeg

½ cup fresh orange juice

Non-stick cooking spray

4 scoops vanilla non-fat frozen yogurt, *or* flavor of your choice

S lice pineapple and refrigerate until ready to grill.
Brown Sugar-Orange Juice Mopping Sauce: In small bowl, combine sugar, cinnamon, nutmeg, and orange juice.

Spray a grill rack and place it on grid over ashen-hot coals. Set pineapple slices on grill rack and brush liberally with mopping sauce. Grill pineapple about 3 minutes on each side, turning once with long-handled spatula. Mop pineapple when you turn it. Pineapple should be hot and juicy.

Remove pineapple to dessert plates. Put a scoop of frozen yogurt in center of pineapple and serve immediately.

You might want to scatter a few tablespoons of orange peel over the hot coals as the pineapple grills for a slight aromatic flavoring.

Nutritional Data

PER SERVING		EXCHANGES	
Calories	204	Milk	0.0
% Calories from fat	2	Veg.	0.0
Fat (gm)	0.4	Fruit	0.5
Sat. Fat (gm)	0	Bread	2.5
Cholesterol (mg)	0	Meat	0.0
Sodium (mg)	61	Fat	0.0
Protein (gm)	3.4		
Carbohydrate (gm)	48		

PEACH SLICES WITH RASPBERRY SAUCE

Many fresh fruits grill well. You really only want to heat them up. With the addition of an interesting topping, one creates a noteworthy and delicious dessert. One might not start the grill just for a dessert, but as long as you are grilling anyway, why not do a dessert too?

Makes 4 servings

Raspberry Sauce
- ¼ cup raspberry fruit preserves spread
- 1 cup non-fat ricotta cheese
- ¼ cup light sour cream

Fruit
- 4 large, ripe peaches, peeled, sliced
- 1 cup fresh raspberries, washed, drained
- Non-stick cooking spray

Raspberry Sauce: Using a food processor or bowl and whisk, mix together preserves, cheese, and sour cream. Spoon sauce into small glass bowl. Cover and refrigerate until needed. Stir before serving.

Fruit: To peel peaches, submerge them in boiling water about 30 seconds or until skin separates from peach. Transfer peaches immediately under cold running water and rub off skins. Cut peaches in half, discard stones, and slice.

Spray a grill rack and place it on grid over ashen-hot coals. Grill peach slices about 4 minutes, turning as necessary with long-handled spatula. Peaches should be juicy and hot.

Remove peaches to dessert dishes. Spoon sauce over peaches, and scatter raspberries on top. Serve immediately.

Nutritional Data

PER SERVING		EXCHANGES	
Calories	156	Milk	0.0
% Calories from fat	4	Veg.	0.0
Fat (gm)	0.8	Fruit	2.0
Sat. Fat (gm)	0	Bread	0.0
Cholesterol (mg)	9	Meat	1.0
Sodium (mg)	38	Fat	0.0
Protein (gm)	9.4		
Carbohydrate (gm)	31.8		

GRILLED BANANAS FOSTER AND YOGURT

Visitors to New Orleans come home raving about a dessert called Bananas Foster. This is bananas cooked in butter, brown sugar, rum, and spices and topped with ice cream. It is a good dessert to adapt for the grill because bananas stand up well to high heat.

Makes 4 servings

Foster Sauce

- 1 teaspoon butter, *or* margarine
- ¼ cup, packed, dark brown sugar
- 1 tablespoon dark rum
- ¼ teaspoon ground cinnamon
- ⅓ cup pineapple juice

Bananas

- 4 small bananas, peeled, cut lengthwise
- ¼ cup fresh orange, *or* pineapple juice
- Non-stick cooking spray

- 4 scoops vanilla, *or* chocolate, non-fat yogurt

Foster Sauce: Melt butter in small saucepan. Add remaining sauce ingredients and cook only until mixture heats. Set aside to serve hot.

Brush bananas with orange juice.

Spray a grill rack and place it on grid over ashen-hot coals. Put bananas on rack, and grill 2 to 3 minutes on each side. Bananas should be hot but not mushy.

Working quickly, remove bananas and put them on individual dessert dishes. Spoon hot Foster sauce over them, and top with scoop of non-fat yogurt. Serve immediately.

Nutritional Data

PER SERVING		EXCHANGES	
Calories	290	Milk	0.0
% Calories from fat	5	Veg.	0.0
Fat (gm)	1.5	Fruit	2.0
Sat. Fat (gm)	0.8	Bread	2.5
Cholesterol (mg)	3	Meat	0.0
Sodium (mg)	71	Fat	0.0
Protein (gm)	4.3		
Carbohydrate (gm)	65.8		

GRILLED FIGS WITH VANILLA-MINT YOGURT

Grilled desserts are usually cooked after you have grilled your entree. Fruits do well on coals that are waning, so it is not necessary to add more coals to the fire.

Makes 4 servings

- 2 cups non-fat vanilla yogurt
- ¼ cup freshly chopped mint leaves
- 8 fresh figs, washed
- Non-stick cooking spray

Put vanilla yogurt in small bowl. Mix in chopped mint leaves. Cover and refrigerate until ready to serve. Stir mixture before using.

Spray grill rack and place it on grid over ashen-hot coals. Cut a small "x" on top of each fig to open it.

Place figs on rack and grill about 2 minutes on each side. Figs should be warm.

Spoon a pool of vanilla-mint yogurt on each plate. Stand fig in center and serve.

Nutritional Data

PER SERVING		EXCHANGES	
Calories	185	Milk	0.0
% Calories from fat	2	Veg.	0.0
Fat (gm)	0.3	Fruit	1.0
Sat. Fat (gm)	0.1	Bread	2.0
Cholesterol (mg)	0	Meat	0.0
Sodium (mg)	57	Fat	0.0
Protein (gm)	3.8		
Carbohydrate (gm)	43.3		

GRILLED FRUIT WITH RASPBERRY SAUCE

After you barbecue, grill some fruit and serve it with a tasty, no-cook dressing, as in this recipe.

Makes 6 servings

Raspberry Sauce

 1 cup non-fat sour cream
¼ cup fat-free mayonnaise
¼ cup raspberries, picked over
 3 tablespoons Chambord liqueur

Fruit

 1 small cantaloupe, peeled, seeded, sliced
 1 pear, cored, sliced
 1 banana, sliced lengthwise, cut into quarters
 2 plums, pitted, sliced
 1 apple, cored, sliced
    Butter-flavored non-stick cooking spray

Raspberry Sauce: In small bowl, mix together sour cream, mayonnaise, raspberries, and liqueur. Set aside in refrigerator.

Fruit: Prepare all fruit and have it handy near grill. Spray grill rack and place it on grid over ashen-hot coals.

Spray fruit lightly. Grill fruit on rack for a few minutes only, turning it once or twice as it heats. Fruit should be hot and soft but not mushy.

Use a long-handled spatula to transfer fruit to individual plates. Drizzle sauce over fruit and serve.

Nutritional Data

PER SERVING		EXCHANGES	
Calories	181	Milk	0.0
% Calories from fat	3	Veg.	0.0
Fat (gm)	0.7	Fruit	3.0
Sat. Fat (gm)	0.1	Bread	0.0
Cholesterol (mg)	0	Meat	0.0
Sodium (mg)	194	Fat	0.0
Protein (gm)	4.9		
Carbohydrate (gm)	40.2		

10.

FOURTH OF JULY FEAST

Skewered Shrimp and Cherry Tomatoes

Chickpeas and Carrot Salad

Grilled Salmon Steaks with Bell Pepper Sauce

Rosemary Potato Wedges with Salsa

Blueberry Summer Pudding

Almost everyone has an early recollection of how the Fourth of July was celebrated in his or her home town. I remember how my father provided fireworks for the neighborhood and what my mother prepared for dinner. She would say: "There should be red, white, and blue food." Usually it would be salmon, mashed or baked potatoes, and a blueberry cobbler or pie for dessert. Now, with the popularity of the grill, the following five recipes, which constitute a family meal, might be appropriate. Thanks, mom, for the idea.

Making your Fourth of July meal on the grill presents some logistics problems that would not occur in your inside kitchen. But, as always, the secret of unchaotic meals is to prepare as much as possible ahead of time. In this case, you can skewer the shrimp, make its chili mop, and refrigerate both in the morning. The salad and red salsa for the potatoes can also be prepared in advance, and the potatoes themselves scrubbed and parboiled. As for the blueberry pudding, it should be made the day before.

When it's time to start your grill on the Fourth, first prepare the bell pepper sauce for the salmon and refrigerate it until needed. Next grill the skewered shrimp appetizers and get everyone started while you put on the potato wedges. After they're cooking, add the salmon steaks to the grill so both dishes are done together. Retrieve the sauces from the fridge, serve up the salad—and let the feast begin!

177

SKEWERED SHRIMP AND CHERRY TOMATOES

Makes 4 servings

Chili Mopping Sauce
- ½ cup chili sauce
- ½ teaspoon Worcestershire sauce
- 1 tablespoon fresh orange juice

Shrimp
- 4 short skewers
- ¾ lb. jumbo shrimp, peeled, deveined
- 1 orange, sliced thin
- 8 cherry tomatoes
- Non-stick cooking spray

Chili Mopping Sauce: Combine all ingredients in small glass bowl. Set aside until ready to use. Stir sauce before using.

Shrimp: Thread shrimp onto skewers, alternating with orange slices and tomatoes, and ending with shrimp.

Spray grill rack and place it on grid over ashen coals. Mop shrimp amply, and grill kabobs 2 minutes. Turn and mop kabobs. Grill 2 to 3 minutes longer or until shrimp are white in color and just firm to the touch. Do not overgrill or shrimp will become tough.

Place one kabob on each plate and pass remaining mopping sauce.

Nutritional Data

PER SERVING		EXCHANGES	
Calories	127	Milk	0.0
% Calories from fat	7	Veg.	0.0
Fat (gm)	1	Fruit	0.5
Sat. Fat (gm)	0.2	Bread	0.0
Cholesterol (mg)	131	Meat	2.0
Sodium (mg)	563	Fat	0.0
Protein (gm)	15.6		
Carbohydrate (gm)	14.3		

CHICKPEAS AND CARROT SALAD

This is an easy and refreshing salad that goes well with a grilled meal.

Makes 4 servings

  2 cups canned chickpeas (garbanzo beans), rinsed, drained
  2 cups grated carrots
  1 tablespoon olive oil
  2 tablespoons balsamic vinegar
1½ tablespoons minced fresh dill
 ½ teaspoon cumin powder
  1 tablespoon sugar
 ¼ cup plain non-fat yogurt

I n a glass or ceramic bowl, toss all ingredients, except yogurt, and cover. Let salad stand for several hours at room temperature. Divide the salad onto 4 plates, and spoon yogurt on top when ready to serve.

Nutritional Data

PER SERVING		EXCHANGES	
Calories	165	Milk	0.0
% Calories from fat	27	Veg.	1.0
Fat (gm)	5.1	Fruit	0.0
Sat. Fat (gm)	0.7	Bread	1.5
Cholesterol (mg)	0	Meat	0.0
Sodium (mg)	370	Fat	0.5
Protein (gm)	5.4		
Carbohydrate (gm)	25.7		

GRILLED SALMON STEAKS WITH BELL PEPPER SAUCE

I do not know where the tradition of serving salmon on the Fourth of July originated, but it is a good idea. It tastes delicious and is readily available at fish markets during the summer. Salmon comes from both coasts.

Makes 4 servings

Bell Pepper Sauce

    Non-stick cooking spray

2 red bell peppers

2 tablespoons fresh lemon juice

½ teaspoon each ingredient: tarragon and thyme

¼ teaspoon salt

¼ teaspoon white pepper

½ cup plain non-fat yogurt

Salmon

½ cup dried thyme for sprinkling on coals for aromatic, soaked in water 5 minutes, drained

4 salmon steaks, about 6 ozs. each

4 slices white bread, toasted on grill just before serving

Spray grill rack and place it on grid over ashen-hot coals. Roast peppers 8 to 10 minutes, turning frequently with long-handled tongs. All sides of peppers should be charred and blistered. Working quickly, put peppers into plastic bag, and close securely with twister seal. Let peppers stand 10 to 12 minutes.

Bell Pepper Sauce: Remove peppers from bag, cut off tops, and remove skins by rubbing gently under cold running water or rubbing skins off with paper towels. Discard seeds. Slice peppers and puree in food processor or blender. Add remaining sauce ingredients and puree. Refrigerate sauce until needed, but serve at room temperature.

Salmon: Sprinkle drained thyme over hot coals. Spray fish lightly with non-stick cooking spray and place it over grid on sprayed grill rack. Coals should be ashen hot. Grill salmon about 4 minutes, turn, and, depending on thickness of fish, grill until done to taste, about 10 minutes in all. Serve salmon on individual dishes over toast, with sauce spooned over fish.

Nutritional Data

PER SERVING		EXCHANGES	
Calories	249	Milk	0.0
% Calories from fat	25	Veg.	0.5
Fat (gm)	6.9	Fruit	0.0
Sat. Fat (gm)	1.5	Bread	1.0
Cholesterol (mg)	31	Meat	3.0
Sodium (mg)	375	Fat	0.0
Protein (gm)	28.3		
Carbohydrate (gm)	17.5		

ROSEMARY POTATO WEDGES WITH SALSA

The salsa can be prepared a day in advance, and the potatoes can be partially cooked in the morning, for easy managing of your time.

Makes 4 servings

Red Salsa

- 1 red bell pepper, seeded, chopped
- 2 jalapeño peppers, carefully seeded, chopped
- 2 large tomatoes, seeded, chopped
- ½ cup minced red onion
- ¼ cup chopped cilantro
- 3 tablespoons fresh lime juice
- 2 cloves garlic, minced
- ¼ teaspoon salt

Potatoes

- 4 potatoes, about 5 ozs. each, scrubbed
   Non-stick cooking spray
- 1 tablespoon crumbled rosemary
- ½ teaspoon chili powder

Red Salsa: Toss all ingredients in bowl. Taste and adjust seasonings. Cover salsa and refrigerate until ready to serve.

Potatoes: Partially cook potatoes in lightly salted water over medium heat until almost fork tender. Drain. When potatoes are cool enough to handle, cut into quarters lengthwise. Spray potatoes lightly with olive-oil-flavored non-stick cooking spray.

Mix rosemary and chili powder together. Rub potato wedges with seasonings.

Spray grill rack and place it on grid over ashen-hot coals. Grill potato wedges, turning as necessary, until potatoes are crusty and cooked through.

To serve, put potatoes on individual plates, and pass salsa to spoon over them.

Nutritional Data

PER SERVING		EXCHANGES	
Calories	178	Milk	0.0
% Calories from fat	3	Veg.	1.0
Fat (gm)	0.6	Fruit	0.0
Sat. Fat (gm)	0.1	Bread	2.0
Cholesterol (mg)	0	Meat	0.0
Sodium (mg)	155	Fat	0.0
Protein (gm)	4.3		
Carbohydrate (gm)	41.3		

BLUEBERRY SUMMER PUDDING

After so many recipes for the grill, we thought we'd close with a recipe not prepared on the grill but appropriate for Independence Day because it provides the "blue" in the red, white, and blue. It can be prepared a day or two ahead of time and served to top off your grilled feast.

Makes 8 servings

4 cups fresh or defrosted blueberries
¾ cup sugar
½ cup fresh orange juice
  Butter-flavored non-stick cooking spray
16 pieces sliced white bread, crusts removed

Orange Sauce

2 cups fresh orange juice
¼ cup sugar
1 tablespoon cornstarch dissolved in rum,
  Grand Marnier, or orange juice

Stir blueberries, sugar, and orange juice in saucepan and simmer 10 minutes, stirring occasionally.

In a 1½-quart bowl sprayed with butter-flavored non-stick cooking spray, mold bread to fit bottom and sides. Spoon 1 cup cooled blueberry mixture over bread. Layer more bread and spoon sauce over until all bread and sauce have been used or bowl is filled.

Cover bowl with double layer of sprayed plastic wrap. Put a plate on top of bowl and place a weight, such as a full can of food, on top of plate. Refrigerate overnight.

Unmold pudding by running a small, sharp knife around inside edge of bowl and inverting it onto serving plate.

Orange Sauce: Bring juice and sugar to boil in saucepan over medium heat. Whisk in cornstarch and continue cooking until sauce thickens slightly. Cool sauce and pour it into bowl; cover and refrigerate until ready to serve. Sauce is served cool or at room temperature.

Slice pudding with sharp knife and serve on dessert plates. Spoon sauce over pudding.

Nutritional Data

PER SERVING		EXCHANGES	
Calories	296	Milk	0.0
% Calories from fat	6	Veg.	0.0
Fat (gm)	2.1	Fruit	2.5
Sat. Fat (gm)	0.4	Bread	2.0
Cholesterol (mg)	0	Meat	0.0
Sodium (mg)	248	Fat	0.0
Protein (gm)	4.8		
Carbohydrate (gm)	66.6		

INDEX